TASTES
OF
ASPEN

Jill Sheeley

JILL SHEELEY

Tastes of Aspen

Recipes from Aspen and Snowmass'
finest restaurants and caterers.

Illustrated by
RUTH STERN

COURTNEY PRESS
ASPEN

First edition published in 1988 by Courtney Press, Aspen, Colorado.

Second Printing 1989

Printed in U.S.A.

ISBN 0-9609108-1-6

DEDICATION

This book is in memory of Greg Mace, a gentle yet intense man who gave so much of his time, his energy and himself to our community. Many of you will remember Greg as "the man in knickers" who ran the Pine Creek Cookhouse at the Ashcroft ski area. Others of you will know the tremendous amount of work he devoted to Mountain Rescue.

He loved the sport of cross-country skiing and wanted others to share in its beauty. He worked hard at having it recognized as a viable source of entertainment. He called it, "a rejuvenation of the soul."

ACKNOWLEDGMENTS

I would like to express gratitude to the many people who helped make this book a reality:

All of the restaurant owners, chefs and caterers *who gave so generously of their time*.

To the following friends who helped test recipes:

> Fiona
> Theresa
> Helen
> Gwyn
> Shari and Chet
> Sharon
> Ellen
> Martha
> Barbara
> Rachel
> Sandy and John
> "Stitch and Bitch" ladies
> Aspen Activity Center ladies

Ruth *for her wonderful drawings*.

Ed and Jane *for their editing advice*.

Karen Keehn *for her Guide to Wine and Food*.

Curt *for his creativity*.

Linda and the Gordons *for their computer help*.

My family and friends *for their support*.

And to Don and Courtney *for their understanding*.

TABLE OF CONTENTS

PART I • **Aspen Restaurants**

PART II • **Snowmass Restaurants**

PART III • **Mountain Restaurants**

PART IV • Caterers

INTRODUCTION

TASTES OF ASPEN is a collection of favorite recipes from the best restaurants and caterers in the Aspen and Snowmass area. Aspen and Snowmass have some of the finest restaurants found anywhere in the world. The superb cuisine served here is complemented by a unique charm.

Choose recipes that vary from a good all-American eatery to a formal sit-down mountaintop restaurant to a restored 1890's railroad car.

Represented are cooking styles from France, Italy, Germany, Mexico, England, America, Austria, Switzerland, Greece, Hungary, Japan, and China. You'll find dishes prepared by professional chefs trained in Europe and the United States and by those self-taught.

The owners and chefs have carefully selected for you either their own personal favorite recipes or those most often requested. I have included their wine suggestions for your drinking pleasure.

Each and every recipe has been tested and re-tested to ensure successful results. They are calculated for Aspen's altitude of 7,900 feet. In Appendix I, you will find a helpful explanation for conversion to low altitude.

Trying new food is one of life's pleasures. I hope you'll enjoy these wonderful and innovative recipes as much as I have.

Bon Appétit!

Abetone Ristorante

THIS CHIC, NEW YORK-STYLE RESTAURANT IS NAMED FOR a ski resort in Italy.

Northern Italian cuisine is the fare you'll find here. The food is prepared to individual order. It's light and they cook with only the freshest ingredients. The menu is extensive and each evening you'll delight in the chef's innovative specialties. Favorites among customers include: prime veal, homemade pastas and fresh seafood. Health conscious diners appreciate the lighter, less fattening sauces. Lobster Fra Dia Volo is a delicate mixture of fresh Maine lobster, cognac, crushed red pepper, garlic, oregano and a fresh tomato sauce. Devotees love this enticing dish.

The kitchen staff is thoroughly professional and take pride in what they prepare.

Abetone is owned by Dan Surin and Ermanno Masini; two restauranteurs who met in New York City. Skiing and the desire to own their own restaurant lured them to Aspen. They merged their talents and opened Abetone which became an instant success. Masini is originally from the Abetone area where his family owned and operated the restaurant, Casina Rossa.

Authenticity exists here. Perhaps that's why so many Europeans frequent Abetone and feel at home.

The decor is Italian contemporary. It's comfortable and spacious with two large dining rooms separated by tinted glass panels. The walls are covered with a gray wool fabric and strips of mirrors in between for a totally different look.

It's not uncommon to find both locals and visitors meeting for a drink, cappuccino or appetizers in Abetone's large mirrored bar area. It has just the right atmosphere.

Melanzane Parmigiana (Eggplant Parmesan)

SERVES 4

2 Medium sized
   eggplants
Juice of 1 lemon
½ C Pure olive oil
2 C All-purpose flour
4 Eggs
2 C Plain bread
   crumbs
Salt and pepper to taste
¼ C Milk
12 Slices fresh
   Mozzarella cheese
Grated, imported
   Parmigiano
   (Parmesan) cheese

Prepare the eggplant: peel and slice each into 6 slices between ¼" and ⅜" thick. Lay slices on paper towels and sprinkle with salt and a generous amount of lemon juice. Let stand 1 hour. Prepare the sauce: sauté onions in oil until transparent, add chopped tomatoes and next 5 ingredients.

■ Pat each eggplant slice dry. Beat the eggs, milk and pinch of pepper. Coat each slice one by one with flour, draw through the eggs and coat with bread crumbs until no bare spots are noticed. Heat ½ cup of olive oil in a large thick-bottomed frying pan until hot but not smoking. Brown the eggplants on both sides and remove from pan placing them on paper towels to soak any excess oil.

SAUCE
1 T Chopped onion
¼ C Extra virgin olive oil
1 16 ounce can peeled pear
   tomatoes
1 t Dried Greek oregano
Pinch crushed red peppers
1 T Chopped fresh parsley
1 t Sugar
½ t Salt

■ To assemble: into a large pyrex baking dish (it should be large enough to accommodate all the eggplant), spoon enough of the sauce to cover the bottom. Arrange the eggplants onto the sauce overlapping as necessary. Cover each slice with Mozzarella and cover lightly with ½ of the remaining sauce. Sprinkle with grated Parmigiano and place in a preheated 375 degrees oven for 30 minutes or until the whole dish is bubbling and the cheese has started to brown. Serve immediately with extra Parmigiano and extra sauce on the side.

Wine Suggestion: Pinot Grigio, Collio Livon 1985.

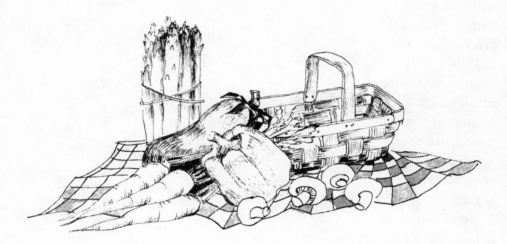

Red Snapper Alla Livornese

SERVES 4

4 8 oz Filets of
   American Red
   Snapper, skinless
1 C All-purpose flour
   seasoned with salt
   and pepper
2 Whole Eggs
1 C Milk
1 Small white onion,
   thinly sliced
8 Fresh pear tomatoes,
   peeled and sliced
1 T Parsley, chopped
Pinch crushed red
   pepper
¼ C Extra Virgin
   Italian olive oil

Prepare the fish: beat eggs lightly, add milk and a teaspoon of olive oil. Dip fish in batter then dredge in flour. Heat remaining oil in a heavy skillet over medium heat, brown fish on both sides (3 minutes per side). Add onions and cook until soft. Add tomatoes, red pepper, and salt to taste and cook 5 minutes more. Place in a baking dish and cook in a pre-heated oven at 350 degrees for 15 minutes. Sprinkle parsley on top and serve with your favorite vegetable or pasta.

Wine Suggestion: Gavi, Principessa Villa Banfi, 1985.

The Aspen Mine Co.

THEIR NAME REFLECTS THE RESTAURANT'S IMAGE. THEY represent the time frame of the silver boom era when Aspen prospered and flourished. Barn wood on the walls is the background for old miners' tools, artifacts and prints of yesteryear. Tiffany-style stained glass lamps hang above the tables and lush plants thrive in the front room.

The Aspen Mine Co. is known for its outdoor patio on the sunny side of the Hyman Avenue Mall. Customers can take in all the sights and sounds of our bustling town.

The menu has something for everyone and their intention is to serve large, quality portions at a decent value. Breakfast is served throughout lunch and there's a large variety of egg dishes. Eggs Mine Company is the most popular. It is poached eggs on an English muffin with artichoke hearts and Alaskan King Crab meat, topped with homemade hollandaise sauce. Lunch offers sandwiches, burgers, soups and exceptionally large, fresh salads. The dinner entrées have fun names: The 49'er (Colorado prime rib), The Miner's Stake (teriyaki sirloin), The Gold Strike (stuffed chicken breast) and The Miner's Catch (Rocky Mountain trout).

They offer a variety of wines by the glass, or you can choose from 14 specialty drinks. Favorites are the Mine Company Colada (a blended mixture of fresh banana, Irish creme, cream de cocoa and pineapple juice) and Mine Company Coffee (Bailey's and Grand Marnier in coffee topped with whipped cream).

The Mine Co. is a cheerful place for families and relaxing for couples. It's as casual as Aspen was in the old mining days.

Chicken Fontina "Gold Strike"

SERVES 4

4 Chicken breasts
1 C Broccoli, chopped
½ C Swiss cheese, grated
½ C Cheddar cheese, grated
Pinch pepper and curry powder
6 Eggs, beaten well
Seasoned bread crumbs
Oil

Remove skins from chicken breasts. Lay plastic film over breasts and pound. Mix the broccoli and cheeses well and season with pepper and curry to taste. Form each breast around the filling (½ cup per breast) then dip in egg wash and roll in bread crumbs. Use toothpicks to hold together. Deep fry until golden brown. Place in oven at 350 degrees for 25 minutes.

Wine Suggestion: Robert Mondavi, Fumé Blanc or Sequoia Grove, Chardonnay.

French Onion Soup

SERVES 20

1 Gallon water
10-12 Medium yellow
   onions, sliced
1 C Sherry
8 Beef bouillon cubes
8 Chicken bouillon
   cubes
Pinch basil
Pinch pepper
Toast slices
Swiss cheese

Sauté the onions in sherry. In a large pot, add water, beef and chicken bouillon cubes to taste. Season with basil and pepper. Simmer on very low heat for 1 ½ hours uncovered. Place soup in bowls, top with toast, then a slice of Swiss cheese and place under broiler until the cheese melts. Serve immediately.

Bentley's at The Wheeler

BENTLEY'S CLAIMS THE CORNER SPOT OF THE NEWLY renovated Wheeler Opera House. This historic red brick building is a landmark in Aspen dating back to 1889. It was built at the height of the silver boom by mining entrepreneur, Jerome B. Wheeler.

Aspen enjoyed four glorious years of performances in The Wheeler before the silver panic hit in 1893. The Opera House also survived two fires in 1912. Walter Paepcke and Herbert Bayer transformed the damaged Wheeler into Aspen's premier theatre once again in 1960. One final, historic face-lift took two years to complete with a gala opening in May 1984. It closely resembles The Wheeler of yesteryear.

Bentley's is owned by Sirous Saghatoleslami who designed the interior with visions of keeping it harmonious with the Aspen Victorian style. It also fits the old/new image of the Opera House. Victorian curtains and lamps, green velvet chairs and English pictures on the walls help to create a warm ambiance. It has the feeling of an English pub. The large mirror behind the bar reads "Bentley's Yorkshire Breweries, Ltd."

Bentley's serves lunch, dinner and late-night snacks. Lunch features fish and chips, seafood crêpes, a steak sandwich, soups, salads and omelettes. Dinner includes prime rib, baby back ribs, salmon, pork chops and gourmet pizza. A variety of imported beers is served.

Bentley's is frequented by both locals and tourists alike. After a concert, play or dance performance at The Wheeler, Bentley's is a must. They go together.

Barbecue Ribs

SERVES 4

2 Racks Baby back pork
  ribs
Powdered barbecue spice

SAUCE
1 T Drippings
1 T Red vinegar
1 T Worcestershire
¼ C Lemon juice
½ C Water
1 C Chili sauce
1 t Brown mustard
2 T Brown sugar
1 t Hickory smoke
  flavor
Salt and pepper to taste

Mix sauce ingredients together. Cook ribs in ¼ inch water in a large baking dish. Sprinkle powdered barbecue spice on ribs. Cover with foil and place in 250 degrees oven for 3 hours. Baste with sauce on charbroiler until crispy and golden brown.

London Pan

2 oz Clarified butter
½ C White wine
2 oz Snow crab meat,
   shredded
6-7 Sea Scallops
2 Large shrimp,
   cleaned and deveined
   or handful of bay
   shrimp
¼ C Tomatoes, chopped
¼ C Mushrooms, sliced
¼ C Green onions,
   chopped
1 t Seafood or lobster
   base
Dash of salt, white
   pepper, garlic salt
½ t Garlic, chopped

Sauté the seafood in the butter and wine and cook until the scallops turn white and the shrimp turn red. Add the remaining ingredients and cook for 3 minutes. Serve over toasted English muffins. This also makes a wonderful filling for crêpes or omelettes.

Charlemagne

ULTIMATELY, YOU SEEK OUT A RESTAURANT BECAUSE of its food. But Charlemagne offers you so much more. Victorian ambiance and professional attentive service are also appreciated by their patrons. They're located in a 100-year-old home on Main Street that belonged to the owner of the Midland Railroad. The lighted trees that surround the restaurant sparkle and glow on a snowy evening and welcome you.

Upon entering Charlemagne, you get the feeling of having been invited to someone's home. And that's precisely the impression that owners Howard and Barbara Gunther want to convey. They truly want you to enjoy one of Aspen's most elegant dining experiences.

The restaurant is divided into three newly renovated dining rooms. The "Club Med" room with its French provincial fireplace is relaxing. The "French Room" is romantic with lace curtains, a pink and mauve color scheme and the original Victorian fireplace. The "Garden Room" is octagon-shaped with a tented ceiling. Its visual appearance, with plants, flowers and a fountain, is striking.

Chris Blachly, a certified professional chef, leads the kitchen in their creative endeavors. His approach utilizes the classic French techniques which he applies in a style all his own. This gives him the freedom to be original and to create new and exciting dishes. He is constantly experimenting. The results are the praises heard nightly from Charlemagne's delighted customers.

Charlemagne's famous salad with hot Brie dressing is prepared table side and the savory aromas fill the air. Homemade desserts are lavishly displayed on a large cart. Coffee and dessert are a must.

The restaurant is very wine oriented, as evidenced by the many picture frames of wine labels on the walls. They have a very extensive wine list (175 different wines) that constantly changes throughout the year in order for it to stay current.

Michael Steinhart has been the sommelier for the past six years. Wine is his love, his hobby and now his business. He has a unique situation at Charlemagne—the Gunthers have given Steinhart full rein, due to his knowledge and expertise. He handles all facets of his self-contracted wine business within the restaurant. Says Steinhart, "People rely on my opinion. If I can make our customers' wine drinking experience more enjoyable, that's my thrill."

Patrons are waited on by no less than five of Charlemagne's professional staff. Howard or Barbara are there to keep an attentive eye on the proceedings.

This mixture of extra special touches, combined with innovative cuisine, brings diners nothing but pleasure.

Charlemagne Salad with Hot Brie Dressing

Tear lettuce into bite-size pieces. Toss with garlic croutons in large bowl. Warm olive oil in heavy large skillet over low heat for 10 minutes. Add shallot and garlic and cook until translucent, stirring occasionally, about 5 minutes. Blend in vinegar, lemon juice and mustard. Add cheese and stir until smooth. Season with pepper. Toss hot dressing with lettuce and serve.

The kicker: do not use high heat. Charlemagne uses a sterno heater and prepares this salad tableside. The aromas are wonderful!

SERVES 8

1   Medium head curly endive
1   Medium head iceberg lettuce
1   Medium head romaine lettuce
Garlic croutons (preferably homemade)
½ C Olive oil
4   t Minced shallot
2   t Minced garlic
½ C Sherry wine vinegar
2   T Fresh lemon juice
4 t Dijon mustard
10 oz Ripe French Brie cheese (rind remains), cut into small pieces, room temperature
Freshly ground pepper

Venison with Grapes and Green Peppercorns

SERVES 4

8 2 ounce Medallions
  venison loin, or
  substitute beef
  tenderloin, halved
2 C Red seedless grapes
4 t Fresh ginger,
  minced
4 t Green peppercorns
8 oz Port wine
4 oz Balsamic vinegar
16 oz Demi Glace (can
  be found at gourmet
  food shops)
2 T Butter
2 T Oil
½ C Flour
Salt and pepper to taste

Lightly pound the meat and dust with flour, salt and pepper. Sauté in oil and butter in a very hot skillet. Remove the meat to a plate and keep warm. Deglaze the pan by adding the port wine to the skillet scraping the remnants of the meat off the sides and bottom of the pan. Boil liquid down to half.

■ Follow the directions on can of Demi Glace. It should reach a thick sauce consistency. Add the grapes, ginger, green peppercorns, vinegar, Demi Glace, and liquid from pan. Serve over the meat.

Wine Suggestion: 1982 Jordan 'Estate Bottled' Cabernet Sauvignon.

Chart House

THE ORIGINAL CHART HOUSE WAS LOCATED ACROSS from Little Nell's—where the Aspen Square presently is situated. Now, you'll find the Chart House on the corner of Durant and Monarch.

It was started by two ski/surf bums who wanted something to do to support their life-styles. They developed the nautical theme for their decor. All of the handmade tables have an authentic nautical chart laminated into the tabletops and are trimmed with teak to enhance their beauty. Many customers enjoy following a previously traveled route.

The photos on the walls also help to set the mood for this California-style restaurant. They depict a variety of sports from sailing, windsurfing and skiing to climbing, kayaking, rodeo roping and skateboarding. They express the owners' enthusiasm for excelling in sports.

The Chart House is now owned by Pacific Ocean Enterprises who also own 57 other Chart Houses in 17 states. Their premise is based on this motto, "We are friendly people serving quality food in a clean atmosphere." And, indeed they do.

The Aspen Chart House is known for its wonderful warm homemade bread and enormous salad bar with over 60 items to choose from. It's a meal by itself. The menu ranges from seafood to beef to fowl. I was told their most popular items are Hawaiian Chicken, fresh red snapper and prime rib. They also offer lobster, shrimp teriyaki, teriyaki steak, scallops, top sirloin, Filet Mignon and teriyaki beef kabob.

The Chart House is famous in Aspen for serving huge pieces of their rich and delicious Mud Pie.

Bleu Cheese Dressing

MAKES 2 ½ CUPS

¾ C Sour cream
½ t Dry mustard
½ t Black pepper
½ t Salt
⅓ t Garlic powder
1 t Worcestershire sauce
1 ⅓ C Mayonnaise
4 oz Imported Danish
    Bleu cheese

Place first 6 ingredients in mixing bowl and blend at low speed for 2 minutes. Add mayonnaise and blend ½ minute at low speed, then blend for 2 minutes at medium speed. Crumble the bleu cheese by hand into very small pieces and add. Blend at low speed no longer than 4 minutes. It must sit 24 hours before using.

Chart House Mud Pie

½ Package Nabisco
    chocolate wafers
½ Stick butter, melted
½ Gallon Coffee Ice
    cream
1 ½ C Fudge sauce
Whipped cream
Slivered almonds

Crush wafers and add butter, mix well. Press into 9" pie plate. Cover with soft ice cream. Put into freezer until ice cream is firm. Top with cold fudge sauce (it helps to place in freezer for some time to make spreading easier). Store in freezer approximately 10 hours. To serve, slice pie into 8 portions and serve on a chilled dessert plate with a chilled fork. Top with whipped cream and almonds.

Garlic Cheese Croutons

Add garlic, salt, parsley, worcestershire and tabasco to melted butter and mix well. In a large bowl, sprinkle Parmesan over bread. Pour butter mixture over and mix with rubber spatula. Spread out in a single layer on a large baking sheet. Cook at 450 degrees for 5-7 minutes watching carefully so croutons do not burn. Stir twice for even browning. Store in an airtight container at room temperature.

1 C Melted butter or
  margarine
1 T Garlic powder
Pinch salt
2 T Parsley, chopped
1 T Worcestershire
  sauce
1 t Tabasco sauce
6 C Bread, day old, cut
  into bite-size pieces
½ C Parmesan cheese

Teriyaki Marinade

MAKES ABOUT 2 CUPS

5 Green onion stalks
2 T Ginger root
2 Garlic cloves
2 C La Choy soy sauce
¼ C Sherry wine
1 T Cotton seed oil
¼ C Brown sugar
¼ C Granulated white
   sugar

In a Cuisinart, blend first 3 ingredients. Add the next 5 and stir by hand until all sugar is dissolved. Bring to a boil. Cool overnight in refrigerator. Strain into separate container (strain only bulk onion). Great for steaks, chicken or shrimp.

Chelsea's Terrace

EXPERIENCE A BIT OF ENGLAND AT CHELSEA'S TERRACE. Mabel Macdonald, the owner, invites you "to join us on our sunny terrace or in the warm elegance of our dining room for conversation with friends as light and sweet as the crumpets, sandwiches and breads that are taken with it."

The ritual of serving tea with small sandwiches came from England. Chelsea's takes pleasure in continuing this "civilized tradition of respite from the world for a 'spot'."

Afternoon Tea is elegantly served. It arrives on a silver tray with a lace doily. Fruit is served first to cut the sweetness of goodies to come. Be naughty, and indulge yourself with scones, buttered crumpets with honey, homemade spreads, devon cream, lemon curd, cakes, breads and traditional sandwiches. This is all accompanied by a fine selection of teas, of course!

In addition, they serve breakfast and lunch. Their unique crumpet bar is available at both meals, complete with wonderful toppings, butters, jams and sauces. Breakfast features Crumpet French Toast, Deep Dish Waffles and Mum's Oatmeal Apple Pancakes. A devotee brags, "They're the best pancakes on the planet!" For lunch, Northumberland Pie, Eggs Ramekin and Spinach Salad are alternatives to the crumpet bar.

Chelsea's is a cozy restaurant. The wooden tables are decorated with maroon cloth place mats and hand-decorated cups and saucers. The prominent color is dusty rose. Lace curtains and fabric-covered walls set the mood in Chelsea's. The waitresses look quite English with their Laura Ashley-designed dresses.

Guy Fawkes Cake

MAKES ONE CAKE USING A
10" SPRINGFORM PAN

CAKE
2 ¼ C All purpose flour,
    lightly spooned into
    cup
1 t Baking powder
½ t Baking soda
½ t Salt
1 t Ginger
1 t Cinnamon
1 t Allspice
1 C Margarine or
    butter
2 C Oats (quick-cook or
    regular)
¾ C + 2T Dark corn
    syrup
⅔ C Brown sugar,
    packed
2 Eggs

Combine first seven cake ingredients. Cut margarine into dry ingredients to make fine crumbs. Blend in oats. Heat the corn syrup and brown sugar together until bubbly and sugar dissolves. Cool slightly.

■ Blend eggs into cooled syrup mixture. Add all to dry ingredients and blend well. Turn into springform pan, greased and floured on the bottom. Bake at 325 degrees, 50-55 minutes until toothpick inserted in center comes out clean. Meanwhile, make Lemon Sauce.

■ Blend sugar and cornstarch together in saucepan. Blend in cold water and cook until thickened. Add a little hot mixture to eggs. Return to pot and cook 1-2 minutes. Stir in lemon juice, lemon rind and butter and blend. Serve cake warm with Lemon Sauce.

This cake celebrates the gun powder plot to blow up Parliament on November 5, 1605. A heavy, hearty cake.

LEMON SAUCE
⅔ C Sugar
¼ C Cornstarch
1 + ⅓ C Cold Water
2 Eggs
⅓ C Lemon juice
1 T Lemon rind
1 T Butter

Wheat Scones

MAKES 8 LARGE TRIANGLES

2 C All purpose flour
2 C Graham flour
2 T Baking powder
1 t Salt
1 T Cinnamon
1 t Nutmeg
⅔ C Brown sugar,
    packed
⅔ C Margarine, cold
1 C Currants
4 Eggs
⅔ C Milk

Combine first seven ingredients. Cut margarine into dry ingredients to make coarse crumbs. Combine currants with dry ingredients to coat fruit. Make a well in center. Blend eggs and milk well with fork. Pour into well in dry ingredients. Mix quickly and deftly with 2-tined fork until just moistened. Turn onto greased cookie sheet. Pat into a circle ¾" thick. Score into 8 wedges cutting almost to bottom. Bake at 350 degrees, until toothpick inserted in center comes out clean, approximately 20-25 minutes.

Crystal Palace

THE MOOD IS GAY AND LIVELY. THERE'S EXCITEMENT IN the air. It's a show from the moment you walk in the doors of the Crystal Palace.

It's packed with patrons dressed in their finest, waiting to hear owner Mead Metcalf and his staff sing and entertain you.

You become mesmerized by the decor. The Crystal Palace lives up to its name—stained glass surrounds you. The crystal chandelier that hangs in the main dining room is magnificent. The atmosphere of this restaurant and theatre is striking, it's vibrant and it's harmonious. From the moment you walk in, you know it's going to be a special evening.

The waiters and waitresses are all in costume running around taking customers' orders and smiling. In 30 minutes, all 200 guests are served a delicious dinner of prime rib, roast rack of lamb, Duck Bigarade or Shrimp Provençal (prepared in the style of Southern France).

As soon as coffee and dessert are offered, the lights dim and magically, the show begins. Presented is a satirical cabaret revue performed by the waiters and waitresses who just served your meal!

Religion, politics and famous people are all topics for this lively, entertaining show. Many of the numbers will make you laugh hysterically, others will touch you. It's witty and professional.

If you've ever been to the Palace, you'll remember such classics as *The Peanut Butter Affair, Old Farts on Wheels* and *Fairy in the Firehouse.*

Mead Metcalf first came to Aspen as a ski bum and played piano at the Hotel Jerome. He opened the Crystal Palace 30 years ago. The building is over 100 years old and was originally an old mining commission. Metcalf remodeled the restaurant himself. "The whole place is for fun. It's all tongue-in-cheek. It's decorated with crazy old junk from the mining days. The railing is from old wrought iron beds and the wainscoting is from doors of old hotels. The old Maxwell and Model T cars, they're for fun, too!"

It all fits together beautifully. The result is a splendid environment complemented by excellent food and a wonderfully funny show you'll tell your friends about.

Duck Bigarade

SERVES 6

DUCK SAUCE
2 C Beef stock
2 t Red wine vinegar
Pinch salt
1 Orange
½ Lemon
3 T Brown sugar
4 T Currant jelly
2 T Arrowroot
2 T Sherry
2 T Cold butter
⅓ C Triple Sec

ROAST DUCK
3 4-4½ pound
   Ducklings
1 Medium onion
1 Large carrot
3 Celery stalks
1 Orange
Salt and white pepper

Make the sauce: bring the beef stock, vinegar and salt to a slow rolling boil. Squeeze the orange and the lemon. Add the juices, peel, brown sugar and jelly to the stock and bring to a boil. Combine the arrowroot and sherry to make a paste. Whisk this mixture into the sauce and bring back to a boil, then remove from the heat. Add the cold butter and Triple Sec to the sauce and whisk until smooth.

■ Roast the duck: preheat oven to 350 degrees. Remove the neck and gizzards from the chest cavity of the ducks. Cut the orange, onion and carrot into thirds. Place a piece of each and 1 celery stalk in each chest cavity. Place the ducks on a rack inside a roasting pan, breast up, and sprinkle with salt and white pepper. Roast for 3-3 ½ hours until the skin is crispy. Remove from oven and pour off the excess grease. Allow to cool in the pan. Cut the ducks in half and remove the backbone. Remove the breast plate and rib cage. Return to the roasting pan. When ready to serve, place in a preheated 550 degrees oven for 10-15 minutes. Remove from oven and top with the sauce.

Wine Suggestion: Chateau St. Jean, Riesling or Grgich Hill, Red Zinfandel.

Swedish Cream

SERVES 6-10

2 C Heavy cream
1 t Vanilla
1 t Gelatin
¼ C Sugar
1 ½ C Sour cream

Heat the first four ingredients until warm, whisking constantly. Do not boil. Remove from the heat and whisk in the sour cream. Pour into individual serving cups or wine glasses. The remainder can be refrigerated and reheated to be used later. Top with berries of your choice. Citrus and fresh fruits are not recommended.

Dudley's Diner

DON'T MISS EATING AT DUDLEY'S WHILE IN ASPEN. Located at the Airport Business Center, Dudley's has a combination Mexican and American menu. The only good thing that can come from the inconvenience of a delayed flight at the airport—is the fact that right across the highway is a locals' favorite diner. Dudley's serves both breakfast and lunch in an airy, comfortable south-of-the-border setting. When the weather permits, their outside patio under the awning is delightful.

The owners of Dudley's are Paul and Patti Dudley. Paul has owned and operated Dudley's since 1979. Patti, who previously baked up at the High Alpine Restaurant, brought with her some wonderful new dishes and desserts to add to Paul's already interesting menu.

Their specialties include: Belgium Waffles, Huevos Rancheros, Swiss Chicken Enchiladas, Quesadillas and homemade soups and desserts. They are available evenings for private parties whether it be a full-course sit-down dinner, an elaborate buffet, or a cocktail and hors d'oeuvres party.

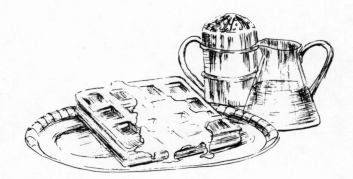

Chicken Quesadillas

MAKES 6 QUESADILLAS

6 *Flour tortillas*
1 *Lb Boneless chicken,*
  white or dark meat
½ C *Canned diced*
  green chilies
½ C *Sliced black olives*
1 T *Chili powder*
1 T *Black pepper*
1 t *Garlic salt*
1 C *Sour cream*
1 *Lb Grated cheddar*
  cheese
Shredded lettuce for
  garnish
cooking oil

Cook chicken by placing in water in a pot, bring to a boil and simmer until done. Drain. Chop into small pieces. Add chilies, olives and seasonings. Stir in ½ C sour cream. Heat a large frying pan or griddle. Brush one side of a flour tortilla with cooking oil. Lay oiled side down in pan. Sprinkle with cheese. Place ½ cup of filling along ½ of the tortilla, fold the other ½ over it to make a "turnover." Continue with the rest of the tortillas, or fry them 1 or 2 at a time, as space allows. Flip them over to brown both sides. Cook until cheese melts and filling is warm. Serve with shredded lettuce and sour cream on top, and Dudley's Green Sauce on the side.

Dudley's Green Sauce

Chop onion fine. Sauté in butter until tender. Add remaining ingredients and simmer ½ hour. Whole or crushed tomatillos may also be used. If using whole, mash or purée the sauce. Use on any Mexican dish.

1 T Butter
1 Small onion
2 Cans (14-16 oz size) Spanish Tomatillos (green tomatoes)
1 C Canned diced green chilies
¼ t Each: black pepper, garlic salt, coriander
½ t Chili powder

Dudley's Huevos

THIS IS DUDLEY'S MOST POPULAR BRUNCH ITEM. SERVES 6

12 Eggs
½ C Half and half
1 C Canned diced
 green chilies
½ Lb Grated cheese;
 cheddar, jack or
 mixture
12 Flour tortillas
Dudley's green sauce
 (recipe precedes)
Sour cream and green
 onions for garnish

Whisk together the eggs and half and half. Scramble eggs in butter in a large frying pan until almost set. Mix in chilies and cheese. Cook until cheese melts. Divide between 6 tortillas, rolling up the eggs inside. Top with Dudley's green sauce, or salsa of your choice. Garnish with green onions and sour cream. Serve with a tortilla on the side.

Patti's Chocolate Dream Pie

CRUST
1 ½ C Chocolate wafer
  crumbs
  (preferably Nabisco's
  Famous Chocolate
  Wafers)
4 T Melted butter

FILLING
3 Eggs, separated
¾ C Sugar
4 ½ Oz. Unsweetened
  chocolate
5 T Butter
2 T Extra strong coffee
2 T Brandy
½ C Heavy whipping
  cream

TOPPING
½ C Heavy whipping
  cream
2 T Sugar
1 t Vanilla

To make the crust: melt the butter, stir in wafer crumbs and press into bottom and sides of an 8" pie tin. Set aside.

■ To make the filling: melt butter and chocolate together. Add coffee and set aside. Mix egg yolks, sugar and brandy in top of double boiler. Over medium heat, beat egg mixture for 8-10 minutes, until thick and pale yellow. Remove from heat. Add melted chocolate mixture. Beat egg whites until fairly stiff. Fold into chocolate. Beat whipping cream until stiff, then fold in. Fill pie shell and chill well.

■ To make the topping: beat whipping cream and sugar together until stiff. Add vanilla. Spread over pie. Can be garnished with chocolate curls if desired.

The kicker: this pie is like a very dense mousse. The recipe can be doubled or tripled or made in any size pan. The pie, without the topping, freezes well for several weeks.

Eastern Winds

ARE YOU IN THE MOOD FOR AUTHENTIC CHINESE cuisine? Eastern Winds is the place to go. It's conveniently located in the very center of Aspen on Cooper Street.

You'll find the owners, Sue and David Han always involved in the many facets of their busy, popular restaurant. Both are pure Chinese. They have created a wonderful, Oriental atmosphere in which to dine. They rejected the traditional red and gold interior of most Chinese restaurants. Instead, you'll find warm, earthy, natural tones. The pictures on the walls are authentic. They were gifts from the Hans' relatives from China.

The menu is extensive with over 100 Mandarin and Szechwan items. Sue explains, "You can get any combination, because we don't premake any of our dishes. It's a very healthy way to eat. With the nature of our cooking, we can accommodate people who have special diets."

These sumptuous dishes are just a few of their many specialties: Crispy Duck, Peking Duck, Volcano Shrimp, Treasures of the Sea and Kung Pao Chicken.

Enjoy one of their many exotic, blended cocktails. A favorite on a snowy evening in Aspen is Tiki Coffee, a delectable combination of Tia Maria, banana liqueur, Amaretto, coffee and whipped cream.

Kung Pao Chicken

SERVES 2

CHICKEN
2 Chicken breast halves,
  boned and skinned
6-8 Water chestnuts, cut
  in quarters
1/4 C Roasted peanuts
1/4 C Sesame oil
1 t Hot chili oil
2 C Vegetable oil for
  frying

MARINADE
2 t Soy sauce
2 t Dry sherry
1 t Cornstarch
1 t Vegetable oil

SAUCE
3 T Soy sauce
1 T Dry sherry
2 T Red rice vinegar
1 t Sugar
1/2 t Cornstarch

AROMATICS
10 Dried red chili pods
2 Green onions, cut in
  1/2" pieces
1 Clove garlic, minced

Whisk marinade ingredients together. Cut chicken into 3/4" cubes and combine with marinade. Mix sauce ingredients in small bowl and set aside.

■ Set wok over high heat for a minute, add 2 cups oil and heat to 300 degrees. Add chicken and stir, to separate pieces. When 90% white on the outside (20-30 seconds), remove and drain. Remove all but 2 tablespoons oil from wok. Reheat. Add chili pods. Stir for 45 seconds, until browned. Add green onions and garlic. Stir briefly until aromatic. Return chicken pieces and water chestnuts and cook 2 minutes. Give the sauce mixture a stir and add it to the wok. Cook until thickened. Sprinkle with sesame and hot chili oils and finally with roasted peanuts. Serve and enjoy!

Mixed Chinese Vegetables

Soak black mushrooms in warm water for 20 minutes. Drain. Remove stems and cut in half. Cut broccoli flowerets into bite size pieces. Slice stems ⅛" thick. Cook broccoli, bok choy and black mushrooms in boiling water for 1 minute. Add remaining vegetables and blanch for 30 seconds. Remove and drain. Combine chicken broth, sherry, salt, sugar and pepper. Set aside. Place wok over high heat for 1 minute, until hot. Add oil. When oil is hot, add green onion and ginger, stirring until fragrant. Stir in chicken broth mixture and vegetables and stir-fry for 1 ½ minutes. Thicken with 2 teaspoons cornstarch paste (made by mixing the cornstarch and water together) and serve.

VEGETABLES
4-5 Dried black mushrooms
½ Small head broccoli
2-3 Stalks bok choy or Chinese napa cabbage, cut into 1 ½" pieces
¼ C Water chestnuts
¼ C Sliced bamboo shoots
12 Snow peas, ends trimmed
12 Canned baby corn, cut in half
8-12 Canned straw mushrooms

SEASONINGS
½ C Chicken broth
½ t Dry sherry
1 t Salt
½ t Sugar
pinch white pepper
3 T Vegetable oil
1 Green onion (white part), minced
1 Thumb-size slice fresh ginger, minced
1 t Cornstarch
2 t Water

The Golden Horn

THE OWNER AND CHEF OF THE GOLDEN HORN IS AN energetic, talented man. Klaus Christ has owned The Golden Horn for 15 years. Originally, The Horn was a "hell-raisin'" bar where famous stars and our own local favorite, Freddie Fisher, played. Presently, The Horn is an Aspen favorite known for its superb continental cuisine with a Swiss flair, and its European atmosphere.

The golden horn, for which the restaurant was named, hangs in the dining room by the fireplace. It's actually a French horn made in the 1890's in Russia. The horn, amazingly, was used in the first Aspen High School Band.

It's a tradition, that during the famous World Cup ski races (held in Aspen), Klaus feeds the Swiss team. Nourishing the athletes these days is a science. Klaus told me, "I consult with the team's coach. It's very important to feed these skiers properly, especially before the actual races." The team is most appreciative and takes Klaus and his wife, Anne, skiing when they visit Switzerland.

Klaus, who is originally from Davos, Switzerland, received his training there by apprenticing in a famous restaurant for three years.

The Horn is well known for its extensive wine list. The present wine cellar has over 8,000 bottles. This is the result of 12 years of studying and collecting wines. "I want to provide my customers with the finest selection of wines that they can find." Klaus has a passion for wine and has invested in rare wines over the years. He points out that a customer should not be intimidated. "I have wines ranging from $14.00 a bottle, to $1,200.00!"

He credits his sommelier of six years, Peter Aldred, as being, "the most knowledgeable wine steward in this town. Wine is his love." The Horn received an award for one of 100 of the best wine cellars in the country.

I enjoyed reading Klaus' guest book, with comments from both local and famous people. This quote stood out from the others and sums up The Golden Horn, "More than artistry in food, a beauty in consistency."

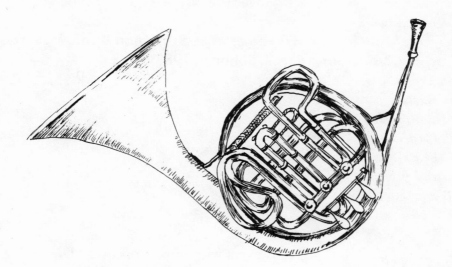

Catfish Golden Horn

SERVES 4

4 Catfish fillets, about 6 oz each
6 oz Butter
1 Lemon, peeled
½ C Capers
1 C Flour
Salt and pepper
1 T Worcestershire

Melt 3 ounces butter in frying pan. Season fish with salt and pepper. Dip in flour and sauté for 5 minutes each side or until done.

■ Remove fish and add remaining butter to pan. Add coarsely chopped lemon, capers and worcestershire and simmer for 3 minutes. Add sauce over fish and serve.

Wine Suggestion: Sauvignon Blanc, Matanzas Creek, Sonoma, 1985.

Parisien Schnitzel

SERVES 4

8 2½ ounce Thin veal cutlets
Salt and pepper
2 Eggs, beaten
½ C Flour
1 C White wine
1 Lemon
4 oz Butter

Season veal with salt and pepper. Dip in flour then in eggs. Heat butter in frying pan, add veal cutlets and sauté each side for 4 minutes. Remove meat and add lemon juice and white wine. Simmer for 4 minutes and pour over meat.

Wine Suggestion: Côte de Beaune 1983 (French Burgundy).

Swiss Onion Soup

SERVES 6

6 oz Butter
4 Large onions, sliced
1 Coors beer
½ C Flour
3 quarts Veal or beef stock
2 Bay leaves
6 Cloves
10 Peppercorns
Salt and pepper
6 Slices of toast to fit serving cups
12 oz Swiss cheese, grated

Melt butter in large pot. Add onions and stir well until onions are limp. Put in bay leaf, cloves and peppercorns. Again, stir well and add flour. Mix well and add beer, then simmer for 4 minutes. Add veal or beef stock and simmer over low heat for 30 minutes. Put in ovenproof cups, lay toast on top and sprinkle cheese over toast. Bake in 400 degree oven for 15 minutes.

Gordon's

ARTISTRY IN MOTION. THAT'S WHAT YOU'LL FIND IN Gordon's fast-paced kitchen. It's abuzz with activity. The staff is an energetic and highly creative lot. It's no wonder they turn out such superb cuisine to a most-appreciative following.

Gordon Naccarato, the owner and motivating force behind this very successful restaurant, came to Aspen from Michael's in Santa Monica, California. It was there that he worked his way up the ranks from a waiter to the head chef. He was persistent and it paid off.

Gordon's literally exploded into the Aspen dining scene. And Gordon has managed to capture the attention of his clientele by changing his menu each evening. His signature dishes remain, yet the opportunity is open for him to create new dishes from the variety of fresh foods he receives daily. Fish comes from both coasts and much of their meat is farm-raised in Sonoma County. Caviar comes from San Francisco, truffles from New York and the tortillas are homemade in Santa Fe. He relies heavily on local growers for the many herbs, edible flowers and unusual lettuces he utilizes. Authentic ingredients are of utmost importance.

What makes Gordon's food so wonderful, so unusual? Matt Stein, Gordon's Sous Chef, describes Gordon's secret of his innovative style of cooking: "Whenever he creates a dish, he consciously strives to balance all the flavors. He wants the dish to touch all of the palate senses. For example, our Swordfish Sicilian-Style—it has the tang from the tomato butter, a savory quality from the beurre blanc sauce, fragrance from the oregano, a meaty taste from the swordfish and a smoothness from the melted mozzarella cheese. Then we added seasoned bread crumbs for a crunchy sensation." All these different consistencies come together for their patrons' enjoyment.

The visual appearance of each plate is impressive. Jumping out at you is a kaleidoscope of colors. There is a harmonious blend of texture, color and taste.

. . . .

Choose from a very large selection of appetizers and hot and cold salads. They're often exotic, outrageous and destined to please. For entrées, it's difficult to decide from the many seafood, poultry and meat offerings. "Kick-Ass" Swordfish is a favorite! Vietnamese Quail is a newly developed dish.

I know it's hard to believe, but most diners save room for dessert. Rebecca, Gordon's wife is famous for her superior and intricate creations. They taste as wonderful as they look.

Eating at Gordon's is sheer gastronomical pleasure.

Goat Cheese Rellenos

AN APPETIZER SERVING 5

5 Anaheim chiles
¼ C Monterey Jack
   cheese
½ C Montrachet goat
   cheese
1 t Shallot, chopped
1 t Garlic, chopped
Salt and pepper
½ t Coriander and
   cumin, toasted and
   ground
1 t Dry sun-dried
   tomato, chopped
2 t Roasted red pepper,
   chopped
½ t Fresh Jalapeño,
   finely chopped
1 T Fresh cilantro,
   chopped
1 t Each: oregano,
   marjoram and
   thyme, chopped
¼ C Cream
2 Whole eggs
Blue corn meal (found
   in health food or
   specialty stores)
Oil
Tomato salsa
Sliced avocado

Roast the chiles until completely charred. Place in a bowl and cover with plastic to steam for 10 minutes. The skins should now be easy to remove. Slit open lengthwise and carefully remove seeds and the bitter white "ribbing." Fill with a smooth mixture of the next 11 ingredients. Mix the cream and eggs together to form an egg wash. Dredge the filled chiles in the egg wash then in blue corn meal. Deep-fry for approximately 1 minute at 350 degrees. Garnish with tomato salsa and avocado.

Wine Suggestion: Storybrook Mountain, Zinfandel, Napa Valley.

Lobster Lasagna

AN APPETIZER SERVING 5

DOUGH
8 Egg yolks
1 C Flour

COURT BOUILLON
½ Orange, chopped
½ Lemon, chopped
½ Lime, chopped
1 Onion, chopped
Pinch thyme
1 Carrot, chopped
1 Celery stalk, chopped
1 Bay leaf
1 C White wine

FILLING
1 Lobster (1 ½ lbs)
8 oz Cream cheese
1 Shallot, chopped
Salt and pepper
3 Cloves garlic, minced
Fresh Parmesan cheese, grated
2 C Mushrooms
Olive oil
1 T Garlic, blanched and chopped
¼ C Red pepper, chopped and roasted
⅛ C Niçoise olives, remove stones and chop
⅛ C Sun-dried tomatoes, chopped
⅛ C Red onion, finely sliced
1 T Each: fresh thyme, marjoram, chives, Italian parsley, chopped
2 T Fresh basil
Whole milk Mozzarella cheese, grated
Chives (for garnish)

GOAT CHEESE SAUCE
1 Pint Heavy cream
4 ½ oz Montrachet goat cheese
1 t Garlic, chopped
1 t Shallot, chopped
Salt and pepper to taste

Recipe continued on the following page

Make the dough: place the egg yolks in a mixing bowl with dough hook on medium speed. Add the flour and mix until it forms a ball. Remove and knead by hand until smooth. Roll through a hand pasta machine starting on 1 through 2,3,4 and twice on 5. Cut into five 6" squares and cook in boiling salted water until tender (about 3-4 minutes). Transfer to a bowl of ice water to stop cooking. Then take it to a work table and trim each into a neat square.

■ Mix court bouillon ingredients in a large stock pot (large enough for the lobster) filled with water. Boil. Poach lobster rare (3-4 minutes). Remove meat and cut into bite-size pieces.

■ Mix next 4 filling ingredients together and spread each square with ¼" of this mixture. Sprinkle with Parmesan. Briefly sauté the mushrooms in olive oil, then cool. Mix the next 7 ingredients together with the mushrooms. On ½ of each square, place 4 tablespoons of the above mixture. Distribute the lobster meat evenly onto the squares. Fold each square over into a triangle and top with grated Mozzarella. Brown slowly under a salamander or in an oven to heat thoroughly.

■ Make the sauce: bring all sauce ingredients to a boil. Remove from heat and keep warm. To serve: place a very shallow pool of this sauce on 5 plates. Place 1 pasta square on each plate on the sauce. Top with chives.

The kicker: although this recipe is time-consuming and requires searching for special ingredients, it's well worth the effort. Each bite bursts with flavor!

Wine Suggestion: 1985 Domaine Michel, Chardonnay, Sonoma County.

Sopa de Pollo

(MEXICAN-STYLE
CHICKEN SOUP)

SERVES 6

SOUP

1 Small fryer chicken,
   whole
1 Onion, chopped with
   skin on
1 Carrot, finely sliced
2 Celery stalks, finely
   sliced
2 Garlic heads, cut in
   half
1 Bunch cilantro (save
   a bit)
2 Bay leaves
1 T Whole coriander
1 T Whole cumin
1 t Each: whole dry
   thyme, oregano,
   marjoram
1 Jalapeño, sliced

Place the chicken in a 1-gallon stock pot and cover with water. Then add the rest of the soup ingredients. Bring to a boil, cover and remove from fire and allow to sit for 5 hours to steep. Make the garnish: slice the first 6 ingredients into strips and grill them, then dice. Dice and sauté the carrot and celery.

■ Reheat soup and adjust seasonings—salt, pepper, lime juice, cilantro, thyme and marjoram. To serve: distribute garnish vegetables and chicken meat in warm bowls. Pour broth over and top hot soup with grated cheeses and fried tortillas.

GARNISH

1 Red onion
1 Zucchini
1 Yellow squash
1 Russet potato
1 Sweet red pepper
1 Fresh Anaheim chile
1 Carrot
1 Celery stalk
Chicken meat, shredded
Fresh lime juice
Cilantro
Parmesan and
   Monterey Jack cheeses,
   grated
Corn tortillas, sliced
   and fried

The Grand Finale

THE GRAND FINALE IS NEXT DOOR TO THE CRYSTAL Palace. It's owned by Mead Metcalf and run with the same professionalism as the Palace.

The show, the decor, the food and the performers are all different with a spark all their own.

Each season features a carefully selected cabaret revue of Broadway hits. The Finale has hosted works by Fats Waller, Steven Sondheim, George Gershwin and Noel Coward.

The atmosphere is predominately art deco. It sets the mood for an evening of live music and dance.

For dinner, choose from prime rib of beef, rack of lamb (baked in mustards and herbs), shrimp in tarragon butter, Duckling Hoi Sin (with the classic flavor of China), Cape Bay Scallops (baked in a bechamel sauce with fresh basil and covered with a delicate puff pastry) and the fresh fish of the day.

In the same manner as the Palace, as soon as the last cup of coffee is poured, the waiters and waitresses don a new role as performers. They entertain the audience with enthusiasm and zeal. The singing, dancing, costumes and lighting are perfectly executed. They do a fantastic job in the limited space available.

You'll be amazed at the abundance of talent this small ski town possesses. For an enjoyable evening of fine dining coupled with live entertainment, try The Grand Finale.

Baked Bay Scallops

SERVES 4

1 C Butter, room
   temperature
1 C Bread crumbs
6 Garlic cloves, crushed
2 T Onion, finely
   minced
½ C Fresh parsley,
   chopped
½ T Dried tarragon
   leaves
¼ C White wine or
   sherry
Juice of ½ lemon
Salt and freshly ground
   pepper, to taste
2 T Vegetable oil
2 T Onion, diced
1 ½ lbs Fresh bay scallops
½ lb Mushrooms, sliced

Mix together first 9 ingredients. Form into a roll and wrap with wax paper. Chill the roll until firm, at least 1 hour. Preheat oven to 450 degrees. Grease a shallow baking dish. Heat oil in a large skillet over medium heat until haze forms. Add diced onion and sauté until soft but not browned. Add scallops, mushrooms, salt and pepper to taste and sauté briefly. Scallops can also be broiled. Place about 3 inches from heat and broil until bubbly, 3-5 minutes. Drain off liquid. Arrange scallop mixture in prepared dish. Discard wax paper, slice garlic butter roll and arrange evenly over scallops. Bake until butter is hot and bubbly (5-10 minutes). Serve immediately.

Wine Suggestion: Chateau Olivier (White French Bordeaux) or Cuvaison Chardonnay.

Hot Chocolate Sauce

Heat the first 3 ingredients in a double boiler for about 30 minutes until smooth. Fold in the heavy cream. Let cool and store at room temperature until ready to use. Wonderful over ice cream (heat first if desired) or over any dessert! Any that is left over can be refrigerated.

1 lb Semi-sweet chocolate, chopped
2 oz Brandy
½ C White Karo corn syrup
1 C Heavy cream

The Grill on the Park

THIS CALIFORNIA-STYLE RESTAURANT LOOKS OUT AT Wagner Park and has a great view of Aspen Mountain.

If you happen to be walking around the Mall and smell the exotic scent of mesquite, it's coming from The Grill. Unique to Aspen, this eatery features Exhibition Cooking and serves ribs, fish and chicken cooked over large logs of mesquite wood.

Owned by Howard and Barbara Gunther, who also own Charlemagne, The Grill fills a gap in Aspen's restaurants. You'll find Chicago-style food in a casual, relaxed atmosphere. It's bright inside, with bold purple tables and chairs complemented by beautiful green plants.

Barbara decided on their menu after choosing her favorite dishes from restaurants she loves most in Chicago.

The Grill's chef is Michael Dietrich who is a native Californian. Barbara boasts, "Michael is an innovator with fabulous ideas. And, he's my son-in-law!"

Specialties of the house include: barbecued ribs, steaks—aged prime and served rare, whole Maine lobsters stuffed with bread crumbs and crabmeat, homemade pasta with miniature vegetables, grilled lime chicken and Chinese chicken salad. All of the sauces are homemade and they use only fresh herbs.

The Grill's Double Chicken Breast with Salsa

SERVES 4

½ C Orange Juice
¼ C Lemon Juice
¼ C Lime Juice
¼ C Soy Sauce
2 Cloves garlic, finely chopped
1 T Kosher salt
¼ t White pepper
1 T Sugar
2 t Whole rosemary
1 t Whole thyme
2 C Salad oil
4 Double chicken breasts-trimmed and slightly flattened

Blend all ingredients together well and pour over chicken breasts. Cover and refrigerate for 24 hours. Drain excess marinade from chicken breasts. Sear breasts on a clean hot grill. Move breasts to medium hot area of grill and continue to cook for 10-15 minutes, turning several times and basting with reserved marinade. Serve with spicy homemade salsa.

Wine Suggestion: 1984 Flora Springs 'Napa Valley' Chardonnay.

The Grill's Marinated Skirt Steak Sandwich

SERVES 4

2 Cloves garlic, finely
  chopped
1 Jalapeño pepper,
  seeded and finely
  chopped
3 Limes, juice only
1 C Salad oil
1 T Kosher salt
¼ t White pepper
¼ t Hot chili powder
4 8 oz Center cut skirt
  steaks

Blend all ingredients well and pour over skirt steaks. Cover and refrigerate for 2-3 days. Drain excess oil and cook steaks on a clean, hot grill for 5-7 minutes. Serve on a toasted roll with garlic butter, sliced onions and tomatoes.

Wine Suggestion: 1983 Chateau Potelle 'Alexander Valley' Cabernet Sauvignon.

Hibachi! An Oriental Grill

HIBACHI REPRESENTS THE CUISINES OF JAPAN, CHINA, Indonesia, Korea and Mongolia.

The owners, Sue and David Han, also own Eastern Winds next door. The idea for Hibachi is to involve people in the easy process of grilling their own food. However, the chefs can do the work if one is not in the mood.

The dining room is very simply decorated with photographs from the Orient on the walls. The main focus are the tables—mostly booths with blue-tiled tables and a grill in the center. You have your choice of three different ways to cook your food. The hibachi is an open-flamed grill that gives the food a charcoal-broiled flavor. The teppan is a hot flat griddle where food can be sizzled in its own sauces. Sukiyaki is a method in which all the ingredients are cooked in one pot to make a flavorful soup or sauce. Shabu Shabu is a Japanese-style fondue.

Hibachi's specialties include: Korean Chicken, Ghengis Khan Beef, Lamb, Garlic Shrimp, Scallops Guyi, Peking Duck and Baby Back Ribs.

Sue explains, "The enjoyable part of Hibachi is watching people get involved in their meals. Kids love to cook for their parents. Groups have a ball! We have taken the most popular items from each country in order to please everyone."

Shabu Shabu

SERVES 2

JAPANESE-STYLE FONDUE.
PAPER THIN SLICES OF
CHICKEN, BEEF OR SEA-
FOOD SWISHED IN A POT OF
BOILING BROTH THEN
DIPPED INTO A SAUCE. USE
CHOPSTICKS!

1 *lb New York steak or
other prime quality
well-marbled beef or*
1 *lb Chicken breast or*
1 *lb Seafood (of your
choice)*
½ *lb Napa cabbage*
1 *Bunch green onions*
3 *oz Bean threads*
6 *Shiitake mushrooms*
½ *C Bamboo shoots*
½ *Onion, sliced*
½ *Tofu cake, cut in
rectangles*
½ *lb Fresh spinach*
½ *C Bean sprouts*
1 *Tomato*
*Chicken Broth (enough
to fill the pot you use
twice)*

Thinly slice the meat or seafood you choose to use. Cut all vegetables into bite-size pieces. Give meticulous attention to arranging the vegetables on one platter and the meat onto another. Japanese presentation of dishes is very important.

■ Mix Ponzu sauce ingredients together. To make the sesame sauce, toast sesame seeds in a dry skillet. Grind them well and mix well with other ingredients. Serve these sauces in separate bowls.

■ Fill a heavy pot or electric wok with chicken broth. Start off with some vegetables (not all) in the pot. Swish meat in boiling broth (it takes only seconds) and dip in either of the 2 sauces. Towards the middle of the meal, ladle out this now-seasoned broth into bowls and enjoy as a soup. Add more broth and vegetables as needed. Sake complements this meal very well!

The kicker: the secret to this dish are the sauces. It's a very healthy way of eating.

PONZU SAUCE
½ *C Lemon juice*
½ *C Light colored soy
sauce*

SESAME SAUCE
4 *T White sesame seeds*
3 *T Sugar*
2 *T Soy sauce*
1 *T Shiro miso*
1 *T Sake*
3 *T Rice vinegar*
½ *T sesame oil*

The Home Plate

A TOTALLY UNPRETENTIOUS RESTAURANT WITH SOME of the finest home-cooked meals in Aspen, is located downstairs in the Mountain Chalet Lodge.

Families, locals and tourists patronize The Home Plate. Its casual atmosphere and friendly, prompt service awaits you. If you're really hungry, they have "working man's portions." They also serve kids' portions.

The daily special board always has a different soup, chicken, pasta, vegetarian and fish to keep things interesting. The food is nutritious and hearty—just like Mom used to make! They only serve dinner.

They can accommodate you if you're famished, or on a diet. The menu varies from sandwiches to very large chef or vegetarian salads to pork roast with mashed potatoes and gravy to fresh red snapper. The desserts are scrumptious and homemade.

The owners are Marcus and Connie Schwing. They are involved in all aspects of the restaurant. Newly added is pool side dining. Since The Home Plate is situated at the base of Aspen Mountain, the view complements their superb home cooking.

Broccoli, Mushroom, Walnut Casserole (Walnetto)

SERVES 6

1 C Coarsely chopped walnuts
3 T Oil or margarine
1 Medium onion, sliced
½ lb Mushrooms, sliced
3 C Broccoli flowerets
½ C Water chestnuts, sliced
1 Clove minced garlic
1 T Soy sauce
½ C Sour cream
¼ lb Monterey Jack cheese, shredded
¼ lb Cheddar cheese, shredded
2 C Cooked rice (we use pilaf)

Heat and brown walnuts in oil or margarine in a heavy skillet over medium heat being careful not to burn. Remove, drain and save oil. Add onion and mushrooms to this oil and cook until softened. You may need to add a bit more oil. Add broccoli and cook until tender. Stir in water chestnuts and garlic. Remove from heat. Add walnuts, soy sauce and sour cream. Stir lightly. Line individual casserole dishes with rice. Cover with vegetable mixture and top with a mixture of cheeses. Bake at 400 degrees for 15 minutes.

Wine Suggestion: 1983 Trimbach, 'Gold Label' Gewürztraminer.

Chicken Deluxe

SERVES 2

2 T Margarine
¼ C Slivered almonds
¾ T Flour
10 ¾ oz Can cream of
   mushroom soup
10 ¾ oz Milk
10 ¾ oz Sour cream
½ C Fresh mushrooms,
   sliced
2 oz Sherry
Pepper
2 10 ounce skinless
   chicken breasts,
   pounded
2 T Margarine

To cook Deluxe Sauce: melt 2 tablespoons margarine in a saucepan. Add almonds and brown. Stir in flour to thicken. Add the cream of mushroom soup, milk and sour cream. Stir over low heat until sauce is heated throughout.

■ To cook chicken: melt 2 tablespoons margarine in a saute pan on high heat. Dredge chicken in flour and place in pan. Brown lightly on one side for color and turn over. Add mushrooms, sherry, 6 ounces of the Deluxe Sauce and pepper to taste. Heat until sauce is bubbly and chicken is cooked throughout. Remove chicken to a warm plate and cover with sauce. The left-over sauce is great over mashed potatoes!

Wine Suggestion: 1983 Cuvaison, 'Napa Valley' Chardonnay.

Chocolate Mint Pie

PIE
¾ C Blanched sliced
   almonds
1 ½ C Shredded coconut
⅛ C Sugar
4 T Margarine, melted
½ Gallon Mint
   chocolate chip ice
   cream, softened we
   recommend "Nabisco
   Mint Oreo"

FUDGE SAUCE
2 oz Chocolate
   (Ghiradelli, semi-
   sweet if possible)
9 T Margarine
½ C Sugar
2 Eggs, beaten

Finely chop almonds in Cuisinart. Combine all pie ingredients (except ice cream) and mix well until moist. Press into 9" pie pan, greased. Bake at 350 degrees for 15-20 minutes or until golden brown. Remove from oven and place in freezer. When cool, fill shell with softened mint ice cream. Return to freezer for 2 hours.

■ Make fudge sauce: melt chocolate in a double boiler. Melt margarine in a saucepan. Combine all ingredients in a mixing bowl and stir until smooth. Put in refrigerator until cool and thickened. Do not freeze. When cool, spread on frozen mint pie.

Hotel Lenado

BREAKFAST IS DIFFERENT AND DELICIOUS EVERYDAY AT the Hotel Lenado. The coffee is hot and freshly brewed. The juices are served in wine glasses.

If you aren't staying at the Hotel, you're welcome to come for breakfast. It's a bit of a secret and seating is limited. It's lovely on a summer's morning to sit out on the deck and take in that fresh, Aspen morning air. Enjoy reading a paper and relax to a real country-style meal. There is one special each morning. On any given day you might find: omelettes, french toast, waffles, blueberry pancakes or super scrambled eggs. Coffee, juice and fruit accompany your meal. Somehow, each dish is special and has that delicate, home-baked taste. The smells coming from their kitchen conjure up memories of elaborate Sunday breakfasts at home.

The hotel itself should not be overlooked. It was awarded the prestigious Mobile Travel Guide's Four-Star award for 1986. It's a small, cozy, bed-and-breakfast-type hotel. The lobby has an amazing 28-foot fireplace and is furnished with rustic twig furniture. The view from the unusual, cathedral-like windows is of Aspen Mountain. The library is intimate and well-stocked. On the walls are old pictures of the town of Lenado, for which the hotel is named.

Two of the three owners once lived in Lenado, a former logging town near Aspen. Leñado is Spanish and means wooded. They wanted to incorporate many kinds of wood into their hotel. You'll find hickory, hemlock, fir, pine, cherry, apple, birch and willow used in a unique style that flows and fits together beautifully.

Banana-Walnut Muffins

Cream together butter and sugar. Add eggs and beat by hand until smooth. Add bananas, vanilla and orange juice and beat. Stir in dry ingredients (do not sift) and nuts. Bake at 350 degrees for 30 minutes in greased muffin tins.

Note: Mandarin orange sections can be substituted for bananas.

MAKES 24 MUFFINS

1 C Butter
2 C Brown sugar
5 Eggs
4 Ripe bananas,
    mashed
1 t Vanilla
2 C Orange juice
3 C Whole wheat flour
3 C White flour
4 t Baking powder
¼ t Baking soda
¼ t Salt
1 C Chopped walnuts

Hot Artichoke Appetizer

SERVES 8-10

2 Cans (14oz)
  artichoke hearts (not
  marinated) drained
  and chopped
1 C Parmesan cheese
8 oz Shredded
  mozzarella cheese
1 C Mayonnaise
1 t Garlic salt

Preheat oven to 350 degrees. Butter a soufflé dish or serving terrine. Mix all ingredients thoroughly in a large bowl. Spoon mixture into prepared dish. Bake for 25-30 minutes. Serve hot with melba toast or stoneground wheat crackers.

French Toast

SERVES 4-6

3 Eggs
1 C Milk
½ t Cinnamon
1 T Sugar
French sourdough bread

Beat together eggs, milk, sugar and cinnamon with a wire whisk. Slice bread 1 inch thick. Dip in batter and fry on seasoned grill until golden brown. Serve with melted butter and dust with powdered sugar. Fresh fruit can be sliced and served on top.

J.J.'s Grille

NAMED FOR THE TWO CO-OWNERS, JERE MICHAEL AND Josh Saslove, J.J.'s is one of Aspen's newest and most innovative restaurants.

Located downstairs from Esprit, J.J.'s invites you to dine in an atmosphere of casual elegance. White tablecloths, red napkins and shiny wine glasses adorn the tables. Original artwork hangs on the walls. They feature one artist's work at a time in order to create a uniform and consistent feeling.

Suzanne Same, the Head Chef, serves American cuisine. The menu is a collection of California grill cuisine, Santa Fe dishes and New Orleans, Cajun-style food. They offer many appetizers and encourage people to put together their own meals by ordering three or four appetizers, soups and desserts. As in Chinese restaurants, patrons pass these dishes around the table. This concept is new and exciting. It's a lighter and healthier way to eat.

Their more popular appetizers are: baked goat's cheese with roasted garlic and sun-dried tomatoes and stuffed pepper with two cheeses and green chilies with a fresh cilantro salsa. Creative entrees are also served. Choose from a wide variety of items that include: Chinese chicken salad, range-free chicken, lamb rack, veal, salmon and three pasta dishes. An extensive, low-priced California wine list is offered.

Jere Michael, who owned and established The Ute City Banque in 1972, explains J.J.'s philosophy, "We are trying to serve a quality dinner at a fair cost. We've created an interesting menu so that people can experience different tastes and different combinations of tastes. We want our customers to enjoy themselves and have fun. Evening meals should be entertaining as well as offering sustenance." To satisfy a growing number of afficionados in Aspen, J.J.'s offers live jazz on a nightly basis.

Cajun Black Bean Soup

SERVES 8-10

3 C Black beans
1 Hamhock
1 C Yellow onion,
   coarsely chopped
1 C Carrots, peeled
   and coarsely chopped
½ C Celery, coarsely
   chopped
⅛ C Parsley, chopped
1 C Peppers: green, red,
   yellow-in equal parts
6 C Chicken stock
⅛ C Garlic, chopped
⅛ t Turmeric
¼ t Cayenne
⅛ t Caraway seeds
¼ t Basil
1 t Salt
½ t Black pepper
½ t Mustard seed
⅛ t Cumin
4 Bay leaves
⅛ t Fennel

Cover black beans with water and bring to a boil. Cover and let sit ½ hour. Drain and rinse. Saute onion, carrot, celery, parsley and garlic until soft. In a large heavy pot, add sauteed vegetables, beans, chicken stock, ham, peppers and spices. Cook uncovered approximately 1 hour until beans are soft. Cool slightly and puree coarsely in food processor. Add salt and pepper to taste.

The kicker: the longer this soup sits, the hotter it gets!

Wine Suggestion: Cabernet Sauvignon. Clos du Bois, Marlstone.

Conchiglia with Grilled Duck Breast and a Red Pepper Purée

SERVES 8

1-1 ½ lbs Conchiglia, linguini or any egg pasta (fresh, if possible)

4 C Roasted and peeled red peppers

1 Ancho chili pepper (found canned in Mexican sections of grocery stores), or use canned hot chilies

4 C Chicken stock

8 Duck breasts (order from your butcher)

Roast peppers until charred black over grill or gas flame, cool in plastic bag and peel, seed and coarsely chop. Add stock and cook until peppers are very soft. Purée with ancho chili in food processor. Reduce over heat until desired consistency. Serve over cooked pasta. Grill duck breast medium rare, slice thin and serve on purée.

Wine Suggestion: Pinot Noir. Acacia, St. Claire Vineyard.

New Zealand King Klip with Tomato-Onion Relish

Mix all ingredients (except fish) and chill. Bring back to room temperature before serving. Fish is best served thinly cut and grilled.

Wine Suggestion: Sauvignon Blanc. Grgich Hills or Cakebread.

SERVES 6

3 lbs Trimmed New
   Zealand King Klip
   or any moderately,
   dense white fish
6 Ripe Roma tomatoes,
   finely diced
2 Medium yellow
   onions, finely diced
½ C Corn oil
⅓ C Apple cider
   vinegar
2 t Kosher salt
1 t Black pepper
1 T Freshly chopped
   parsley, cilantro or
   mint may be
   substituted

Le Bistro Des Amis

ENTER LE BISTRO DES AMIS AND DISCOVER AN AUTHENTIC French bistro.

Co-owners Jean François Deschamps and Jerry Hinz have created this charming restaurant which was previously The Souper. The decor is French country. The colors are peach and green. Dried flowers adorn the walls and hang from the ceiling. Typical French floral curtains serve both as a backdrop and as an awning over the bar. The tables are close together and intimate. Popular French music plays in the background and temporarily takes you away to a small town in France.

Deschamps, the Head Chef and Hinz felt the need for a new restaurant concept in order to meet the needs of this ever-changing resort town. Together, they decided on a bistro, which they describe as, "a small, intimate, relaxed restaurant, run by professionals, serving great classical provincial cuisine at moderate prices."

The waiters are traditionally dressed. They are professional, but not formal. Many of the waiters, along with Deschamps, speak fluent French, which helps to create the atmosphere. Maybe that's why so many Europeans flock to this tiny restaurant seeking the flavor of their homelands.

Something fun and different that Le Bistro has to offer is paper and crayons on all the tables with which to create your own designs. Deschamps told me that they've found great artwork, along with messages in many different languages.

The menu is extensive in French Bourgeois cuisine and they offer many fine wines, both California and French, to complement your meal.

Deschamps sums up his philosophy, "There is nothing I'd rather do than cook good food and serve great wines for the people of my community. Doing what you do well and naturally, what you're gifted for, is the key to success and happiness."

Bordelaise Sauce for Steaks

SERVES 4

5 Shallots
1 Stick butter
1 C Any good Cabernet
½ C Water
Salt and pepper
4 Steaks

Sauté the shallots' heads, finely chopped in a stick of butter. Add the Cabernet and water. Let reduce for approximately 25 minutes or until most of the water has evaporated and the acidity has mostly disappeared. Add salt and pepper to taste. Place the sauce on 4 grilled steaks at the last moment.

Wine Suggestion: Jordan Cabernet.

Le Bistro Veal Sauce

SERVES 2

2 t Fresh thyme
½ Large sundried
   tomato, finely
   chopped
½ Stick butter
½ C White Burgundy or
   a good Chardonnay
¼ C Heavy cream
Salt and pepper
2 Veal steaks

Sauté thyme and sundried tomato in butter and wine. Add cream. Reduce to a heavy cream consistency. Add salt and pepper to taste. Place the sauce on 2 grilled, medium rare veal steaks at the last moment.

Wine Suggestion: Gevrey Chambertin.

Chocolate Mousse

SERVES 12

12 oz Semi-sweet
    chocolate, preferably
    Ghirardelli
1/4 C Water
6 Egg whites
8 Egg yolks

Melt chocolate with water over double boiler on low heat until smooth, using a whisk—do not overcook. Remove from heat and mix with egg yolks. Beat egg whites until stiff and thick. Be careful not to overbeat. Fold whites delicately with chocolate and egg yolk mixture. Pour into individual glass bowls and refrigerate for a couple of hours before serving.

Little Annie's

BUTCH CASSIDY AND THE SUNDANCE KID WOULD HAVE felt right at home at Little Annie's. It's a "kick off your boots and stay awhile" eatery. This is a fun place. If you're looking for local color, Little Annie's bar has just that. It's always hopping with long-time locals gathering to drink a beer and a shot. It's where the softball teams get together to celebrate their wins or commiserate their losses.

This western-style saloon is owned by Judi Jenkins who opened it in the early 70's. She named it after the Little Annie's mine which is located on the back side of Aspen Mountain. Judi explains. "I wanted the name to have some significance for the town. I wanted Little Annie's to have a western theme—you know, cowboys and Indians. I wanted it to feel good and be casual."

They serve barbecued chicken and ribs, trout, sandwiches, hamburgers, huge salads and Judi's Mom's famous potato pancakes. The wood-burning stove in the dining room always has wonderful homemade soups and chili brewing. The aromas are enticing. Families love Little Annie's. It's precisely the environment Judi chose to create. The food is excellent, the feeling is congenial and the staff (many who have worked there for years) is friendly.

Just a block away, Judi owns and operates the Fry By Night Doughnut Shop. If it's a sweet tooth you have, their doughnuts, muffins and cookies will more than satisfy you!

Halibut Papillote a.k.a. Bob-in-a-Bag

SERVES 2

ORIGINALLY, THIS AP-
PEARED ON THE MENU
UNDER THE UN-LITTLE
ANNIE'S-LIKE, FRIGHTEN-
ING TITLE OF "POISSON EN
PAPILLOTE"—YOU GUESSED
IT, ALIEN FRENCH FOOD
RIGHT HERE IN THE
MIDDLE OF THIS BUFFALO-
ROAMING AND THE ANTE-
LOPE-PLAYING TERRITORY.
SO, WE CALLED IT BOB, PUT
HIM IN A BAG AND HERE'S
HOW YOU CAN, TOO!

2 *7 oz portions of halibut*

2 *Lemons, sliced with peels removed*

8 *Butter pads, ¼" thick*

1 *Red onion, sliced*

White pepper

Salt

Whole dill weed

4 *oz White wine*

2-3 *Egg yolks*

2 *Sheets parchment paper (found in specialty stores), 16" X 24"*

Make 2 heart-shaped forms: fold the parchment paper in half crosswise. Cut from the folded edge to the open edge, a half heart, so that when the paper is opened, a full heart-shape is formed. Allow almost twice as much paper as the size of the fish. Start with 2 lemon slices, place them near the fold, about 3" apart in the center of one side of the paper. Place 2 butter pads next to the lemons. On top of these, place 4 onion slices, dash of salt, white pepper and dill weed. Place the fish on top, then place 2 lemon slices, 2 butter pads, onion slices and spices on top of the fish. With the parchment paper still open, take a pastry brush and paint the entire border of paper with egg yolks. Ladle 2 ounces of wine over the fish and immediately fold the paper in half to match up the outer edges.

■ Starting from either end and working along the open edge, begin folding the paper over in small sections. Continue all the way to the other end until you have one continuous seal. This procedure lets the fish cook quickly and allows all the flavor to remain inside. Repeat this process for the second piece of fish. Bake in a preheated 450 degrees oven for 10 minutes. If sealed properly, the bag will puff up like a balloon. Punch a small hole in it as soon as it comes out of the oven.

The kicker: you'll find that it is much less time consuming and much more enjoyable getting Bob out of the bag than it was getting him in!

Wine Suggestion: Glen Ellen, Chardonnay.

Mulligatawny Soup

SERVES 8

½ Green pepper, diced
  medium
½ Granny Smith apple,
  diced small
⅓ Eggplant, peeled,
  diced small
2 Celery ribs, diced
  small
½ Onion, diced small
¼ Stick butter
½ C Boiled rice
¾ lb Chicken meat,
  chopped
3 C Chicken broth
2-3 t Curry powder (or
  to taste)
3 C Milk
1 ¼ C Cream
Salt and pepper
Flour

Blanch green peppers, apples and eggplants. Rinse with cold water. In a large soup pot, sauté the onions and celery in butter until the onions are clear. Add the curry powder and mix well. Add enough flour to form a roux and cook 2-3 more minutes stirring frequently. Add hot chicken stock slowly while blending well. Let simmer while you heat the milk and cream. Finally, add the milk, cream, chopped chicken, vegetables, apples and rice. Season to taste. For a thicker soup, blend in some more roux.

This is a very popular soup at Little Annie's and has slight variations from recipes you may have seen before.

Potato Pancakes

MAMA TOPOL'S WORLD
FAMOUS POTATO PAN-
CAKES!

SERVES 8

3 lbs Mature potatoes
1 Egg, beaten
¾ T Black pepper
1 ½ T All-purpose flour
¼ Large onion, grated
Oil for frying
Apple sauce
Sour cream

Peel and grate potatoes. Place the gratings on a muslin towel and wring the towel to extract as much moisture as possible. Place the gratings in a mixing bowl. In a separate bowl, combine the next 4 ingredients. Add to the grated potatoes and mix thoroughly. Shape into patties of uniform thickness (¼-½") and fat fry at 350 degrees until golden brown on each side. Serve them hot with apple sauce and sour cream and enjoy a little bit of Chicago that Judi brought to the mountains.

Maurice at the Aspen Alps

P ROBABLY THE MOST INTERESTING THING ABOUT
Maurice's restaurant, beside the superb food, is Maurice himself.
A jolly, extremely amiable gentleman, Maurice exuberates friend-
liness and has a way of making people smile.

Maurice came to the United States from Chartres, France. At the
young age of 14, he apprenticed in a restaurant called Maison L'homme.
"It was very intense, hard labor; carrying coal, polishing copper and
other assorted jobs. We worked 14-hour days, seven days a week for
three years. We learned to make pastries from the chefs; we were never
taught; we simply observed."

Maurice has cooked for such notables as Antenor Patino, Prince Louis
II of Monaco, Philip Rothschild, De Rivera (the Spanish Ambassador)
and Lady Browlo, a British aristocrat. He catered the reception after the
wedding in Paris for Queen Elizabeth and the Duke of Edinburgh.

After living in Denver and cooking in various restaurants there, Maurice moved to Aspen and started his own French restaurant in 1969.
Located next to the Aspen Alps' pool, he specializes in weddings, private
parties and cooking classes. If you've never taken one of Maurice's
famous classes, you're missing an unforgettable culinary experience.

Cold Cream of Tomato Soup

Gently sauté leek and pepper in butter. Stir in flour and cook for a few minutes on very low heat. Add remaining ingredients. Increase heat and simmer for 25 minutes. Remove bay leaf. Purée soup in food processor in batches. Strain twice. Stir in whipping cream. Serve hot or cold.

SERVES 8

¼ C Butter
1 Leek, chopped
1 Sweet red pepper, diced
¼ C Flour
8 Very ripe tomatoes, chopped
½ t Saffron
1 Bay leaf
Salt and pepper
2 Quarts Veal stock
½ C Whipping cream

Crêpes Suzette

SERVES 8-10

CRÊPES
1 C Flour
3 t Sugar
Pinch salt
7 Eggs
2 C Milk
1 t Remy Martin
   brandy
1 T Butter, melted

CUSTARD FILLING
2 C Milk
⅓ C Sugar
⅔ C Flour
6 Egg yolks
1 Stick butter
¼ C Triple sec
1 Orange, zested then
   squeezed

Whisk all crêpe ingredients together. Strain to remove lumps. Let rest for 2 hours then make crêpes. To make crêpes: in a caste iron skillet, lightly butter the pan using a paper towel. When the pan is hot, use a cup with a spout to pour the batter into the pan. Swirl it all around and quickly pour any excess out. Whatever batter sticks to the pan will make a perfectly thin crêpe. Cook until just before the edges turn crispy.

■ Filling: scald the milk. In a bowl, whisk together the sugar, flour and egg yolks. Add the hot milk. Return all to saucepan and bring to a boil, stirring constantly. Boil for 2 minutes, then remove from heat. Gradually whisk in butter, orange zest, juice and triple sec.

■ Fill each crêpe with a tablespoon of custard, spreading it evenly. Fold crêpe any way you prefer. Crêpes may be prepared to this point several hours in advance. When ready to serve, heat oven to 350 degrees. Put crêpes on buttered baking sheet and bake about 8 minutes. Remove crêpes to serving dish or warm plates, allowing about 3 per person. Sprinkle with a little sugar. Gently warm ⅓ cup brandy (in order to flame). Pour over crêpes. Averting your face, ignite brandy with a match and serve.

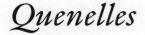

Quenelles

SERVES 8-10

COURT BOUILLON
12 Shrimp shells
½ C Celery, chopped
3 t Shallots, chopped
1 Carrot, chopped
4 t Parsley
1 Bay leaf
3 C Dry white wine
3 C Cold water
1 t Salt

QUENELLE MIXTURE
2 lbs Shrimp, raw,
   peeled and deveined
⅓ t Salt
¼ t Pepper
2 Egg whites
⅔ C Heavy whipping
   cream

MUSHROOM SOUFFLÉ
½ C Butter
2 t Shallots, chopped
5 C Mushrooms,
   chopped
⅓ t Salt
⅔ C Flour
2 ½ C Milk
10 Egg yolks
10 Egg whites
Salt and pepper

HOLLANDAISE
7 Egg yolks
6 Half egg shells of
   water
Pinch salt
⅔ C Butter
Juice of ⅓ of lemon

SAUCE
¼ C Butter
3 t Shallots, chopped
¼ C Flour
¼ C Whipping cream
Salt and pepper

Recipe continued on the following page

Make the court bouillon: combine ingredients in a large saucepan, bring to a boil and cook for 1 ½ hours. Cool slowly, then strain leaving only liquid. Then bring back to a boil (you'll poach the shrimp in this liquid).

■ To make quenelles: grind shrimp very fine. Add next 3 ingredients and mix well. Add cream, mixing over ice. Set aside. Keep cool (over ice or refrigerate) and covered for at least ½ hour.

■ To make mushroom soufflé: add shallots, mushrooms, salt and ¼ cup butter and heat uncovered on medium heat until water cooks off. Add ¼ cup butter and ⅔ cup flour. Whisk while adding the milk. Bring to a boil and set aside. Grease a glass pyrex dish (one with straight sides) with butter (not melted). Add 10 egg yolks to mushroom mixture. Beat 10 egg whites until they peak (add pinch salt to whites). Add mushroom mixture to egg whites and season with salt and pepper. Fold together. Pour ⅔ mixture into pyrex and bake at 450 degrees for 8-10 minutes or until there is a crust on top.

■ Poach the chilled shrimp mixture, by the tablespoon in the court bouillon over a low flame uncovered. Add salt and pepper to taste. Poach for 10 minutes and remove. Set aside. Place quenelles on top of soufflé and add a layer of the soufflé mix on top and bake 5 minutes at 450 degrees.

■ Make hollandaise: whisk in a double boiler over medium heat 7 egg yolks, the water and pinch salt until thick. Add ⅔ cup butter whisking gently, then add juice of lemon and mix well. Do not boil.

■ Make sauce: simmer butter and shallots until colorless. In a separate pan, make a roux of flour and what's left of the court bouillon and bring to a boil. Add whipping cream and boil. Season with salt and pepper to taste. When ready to serve, add 1 cup hollandaise. Serve Quenelles on sauce with fresh parsley, a salad and fresh vegetables.

The kicker: this recipe requires many steps, but is quite easy and very rewarding. Your guests will love it!

Wine Suggestion: Stonegate, Chardonnay.

. . . .

Veal Florentine

SERVES 4

8 Veal scallops,
   pounded to ¼"
   thickness
1 lb Fresh spinach
Pinch nutmeg
Pinch salt
4 oz Butter
2 C Mushrooms, sliced
1 Shallot, diced
¼ C Madeira wine
1 ½ C Veal stock or
   substitute chicken
   stock
1 C Whipping cream
Salt and pepper

Remove stems of spinach and steam with 2 oz butter, nutmeg and salt for 4 minutes. Set aside in a warm place. Lightly flour the veal and sauté in remaining 2 oz of butter until just cooked; set aside again keeping it warm while you prepare the sauce. Drain any excess fat out of pan, then in this same pan, sauté the shallot and mushrooms. Add the Madeira and stock and reduce until about 4 tablespoons of liquid remains. Add cream and simmer until lightly thickened. Season to taste with salt and pepper. Divide the spinach between 4 plates. Top with 2 pieces of veal each. Pour sauce over veal and serve.

Wine Suggestion: Far Niente, Chardonnay.

Milan's Greenhouse

HAVE YOU BEEN CRAVING ITALIAN FOOD LATELY? Tucked neatly away on the garden level of the Wheeler Square Building, far from the mainstream of Aspen's busy restaurants, is Milan's Greenhouse.

Owned and operated by Milan Prikryl, this intimate restaurant specializes in Italian and Continental cuisine, seafood and wild game.

The color scheme is pink and green and somehow suggests relaxation. Large photographs of the Aspen area adorn the walls. Outdoor patio dining is provided in the summer.

I asked Milan why he started this restaurant. He replied with a smile, "I have a family. I love to ski, bike and play tennis. I love Aspen, and this restaurant allows me to share in this beautiful community and make a living."

Milan's Greenhouse has been coined, "the best kept secret in town," by an appreciative following.

Fettuccine Milano

AN APPETIZER SERVING 2

½ C Prosciutto ham
½ C Snow peas
1 T Butter
2 t White wine
½ C Sliced mushrooms
1 C Heavy cream
¼ t Dried thyme
½ t Oregano
¼ t Dried basil
½ C Fresh Parmesan
   cheese, grated
Pinch salt & pepper
16 Oz Fettuccine
   noodles

In a hot sauté pan, cook ham and peas in butter and white wine for 3-5 minutes. Add heavy cream, mushrooms and seasonings. Let reduce until almost thick and add Parmesan cheese. Stir in until it is incorporated in the cream over heat. When it is thick and creamy, pour over cooked fettuccine noodles.

Wine Suggestion: Frascati Pallavicini,1984. An Italian dry white wine.

Pepper Steak

SERVES 2

2 10 Oz New York cut
  steaks, trimmed
½t Shallots
½C Sliced mushrooms
1 C Heavy whipping
  cream
1 T Fresh peppercorns,
  pounded coarsely
½C Brandy
Pinch salt & pepper

Prepare the steaks ahead of time with the crushed peppercorns and let it season itself for a day. Keep refrigerated. Place the steaks in a hot sauté pan and sear both sides for about 9-10 minutes. Remove from the pan and save the juices. Add the shallots, mushrooms and brandy. Ignite the brandy and let it burn for a few minutes. Add the heavy cream and let it reduce until thick and creamy. Add the salt and pepper. Pour over steaks. Serve with boiled, sautéed potatoes or rice pilaf.

Wine Suggestion: Chateau de la Chaize, 1984 (Beaujolais).

The Mother Lode

THE ESSENCE OF THE MOTHER LODE IS REFLECTED IN the large stained glass mural in the main dining room. In the center of this impressive piece, is a large mermaid who is symbolic of the mother lode—a mining term used to describe the source of the gold. On either side, are men attempting to reach this vision.

The owners, Howard Ross and Gordon Whitmer, originally came to Aspen as ski bums. Both worked at the restaurant and eventually purchased it in 1970. Gordon attributes their success to the good food and the fact that, "People love this old building. It feels good in here."

The Mother Lode is one of the oldest buildings in Aspen, going back to 1886. The interior is what you'd expect from a building this old—it's charming and Victorian, with wooden floors and a wood burning stove in the center of one of the four dining rooms. Hanging from the walls are pictures of racy Victorian women, some whose eyes seem to follow you everywhere. Howard and Gordon have been collecting these wonderful women for the past 17 years.

Chef Don Edmonds described "The Lode's" menu to me as a combination of Italian and eclectic cuisine. Specialties include: Veal Parmesan, Veal Picatta, Confit of Duck and Shrimp Scampi. Beside four different spaghetti items, the menu offers eight pasta dishes from the traditional Fettucini Alfredo to Chicken Farfalle (wild mushrooms, chicken breast and prosciutto served on pasta bows). There are also many appetizers and scrumptious desserts to choose from.

The outstanding food, coupled with authentic Victorian atmosphere, makes The Mother Lode a perfect place to dine while in Aspen.

Canneloni

SERVES 6

FILLING
4 Cloves garlic, chopped
1 lb Ground pork
4 oz Prosciutto
2 Onions
1 lb Ricotta cheese
1 C Parmesan cheese
1 lb Fresh spinach
1 t each-salt, pepper
   and nutmeg

SAUCE
½ C Olive oil
¼ C Garlic, chopped
32 oz Canned tomatoes
¼ C Parsley, chopped
1 T Basil
½ T Oregano
½ t Salt
½ t Pepper

PASTA
12 4" X 4" Fresh pasta
    squares (we make our
    own; you can
    substitute manicotti
    noodles)

Sauté first 4 ingredients in butter. Cool completely. Set aside. Wash spinach and remove stems. Steam until thoroughly wilted. Squeeze out all liquid. Chop finely. Cool completely. Mix ricotta, Parmesan cheese, salt, pepper and nutmeg. Stir in pork mixture and cooked spinach. Set aside.

■ Prepare the sauce as follows: cook garlic in olive oil until soft but not browned. Add remaining ingredients and simmer slowly for an hour or more. Cook pasta squares in boiling salted water. Roll pasta around filling. Arrange in shallow baking dish. Top with sauce. Bake in a 350 degree oven until bubbling hot.

The kicker: this recipe also works beautifully without any meat.

Wine Suggestion: Santa Margherita, Pinot Grigio, 1985.

Chicken Farfalle

SERVES 6

4 oz Butter
2 oz Dried porcini
  mushrooms (found at
  specialty stores)
3 C Heavy cream
¼ C Parsley
2 Cloves garlic
2 oz Prosciutto
2 lbs Boneless chicken
  breasts
1 lb Farfalle noodles
  (bow ties)

Soak porcini mushrooms in an excess of water. After they have softened, lift them out of the water and rinse thoroughly. Reserve soaking liquid. Chop mushrooms and sauté in 2 ounces of butter. Add the heavy cream and simmer slowly. Carefully pour the mushroom-soaking water into a shallow pan, leaving any sand or dirt behind. Boil soaking liquid rapidly until reduced in volume. Add this liquid to the porcini-cream mixture and continue simmering slowly until thick. If not thick enough, you may need to add a little cornstarch mixture. Set aside.

■ Wash, dry and chop parsley. Chop garlic very fine. Blend parsley and garlic. Set aside. Slice prosciutto very thin and cut into strips. Set aside. Cut chicken breasts into bite size chunks and cook very gently in remaining butter until just done. Add porcini cream and simmer briefly. Remove from heat. Stir in garlic-parsley mixture and prosciutto strips. Serve immediately over freshly cooked farfalle noodles.

Wine Suggestion: Ruffino Chianti Reserva, Ducale Gold, 1980.

The Paragon

THE PARAGON IS ONE OF ASPEN'S OLDEST CONTINUING food and beverage businesses. The historic building, which today houses the nightclub and restaurant, has always been at the heart of life in Aspen. Constructed in 1885, the building first served the community as a cafe and clothier through the boom years of silver mining. In 1893, America converted to the gold standard and Aspen's boom cycle abruptly ended. The town settled back into a comfortable lethargy that was to last half a century. During this period, the Paragon was to play many roles in Aspen's history. It housed the community grocery store and Dreamland Theater (in the era of silent movies). The Paragon has the distinction of being the first building in the state of Colorado to have electricity. During the 30's and 40's, it functioned as City Hall and served as a venue for the town council meetings.

R.O. Anderson bought the Paragon in the mid 1940's and used the space to feed the music students. He then turned the building into a gourmet restaurant. Ted Koutsoubos bought the Paragon in 1973. He completely renovated the inside to a modern entertainment complex with incredible stained glass throughout the building. The original brick walls bring you back to a previous era of Victorian nostalgia.

Today, as in the past, the Paragon is an active part of life in Aspen. Their lively nightclub offers the finest in contemporary music videos, dancing, live entertainment and the only laser light show in the Colorado Rockies. Dine on their outdoor patio on the Hyman Avenue Mall for breakfast or lunch. Sip one of their famous daiquiris and watch the sunset, or try their oyster bar for fresh oysters on the half shell.

The Paragon is proud to be a vital part of Aspen's past and an integral part of Aspen's future.

Paragon Chili

SERVES 10

¼ C Olive oil
¾ lb Yellow onion, chopped
1 lb Sweet Italian sausage
2 lbs Beef chuck ground
1 T Ground pepper
1 8 oz Can tomato paste
1 ½ T Fresh garlic, minced
1 oz Cumin seed, ground
2 oz Plain chili powder
¼ C Dijon mustard
2 T Salt
2 T Basil
2 T Oregano
2 ½ lbs Canned Italian plum tomatoes
¼ C Red wine
2 T Lemon juice
3 T Fresh dill, chopped
1 16 oz Can dark red kidney beans, drained
1 5 ½ oz Can pitted black olives, sliced

Heat olive oil in large soup kettle. Add onions, cover and cook for about 10 minutes on low heat. Add sausage and ground chuck and cook over medium heat stirring often until meats are browned. Spoon out as much excess fat as possible. Over low heat, stir in next 9 ingredients and mix well. Then add the next 5 ingredients. Stir well and simmer uncovered for 20 minutes. Add olives and simmer covered for 5 minutes.

Wine Suggestion: Raymond, Cabernet Sauvignon.

Paragon Pasta Salad

SERVES 4-6

1 lb Medium size bay
    shrimp
½ lb Pasta (spiral
    noodles work great!)
1 C Peas
½ C Sweet red peppers,
    diced
½ C Purple onion,
    minced
½ C Olive oil
3 T Lemon juice
¼ C Basil
Salt & pepper
1 C Sliced black olives
¾ C Artichoke hearts

Bring a large pot of salted water to a boil. Drop in pasta. Return to boil. Cook until pasta is tender. Drain.

■ Boil water, remove from heat and add shrimp to cook for 4 minutes. Drain. When cool, devein. Toss shrimp and pasta into large bowl. Add peas, peppers and onion. Toss again. Mix olive oil, lemon juice and basil together. Add and toss. Add artichoke hearts and season to taste. Toss again.

■ Serve over bed of lettuce. Sprinkle black olives over top.

Wine Suggestion: Chateau St. Jean, Chardonnay.

Ted's Hot and Spicy Shrimp

SERVES 6

½ C Onion
½ C Green pepper,
    chopped
¼ C Butter, melted
3 T All-purpose flour
1 C Water
1 8oz Can tomato
    sauce
2 Bay leaves
½ T Garlic
½ T Salt
½ T Fresh ground
    pepper
¼ T Paprika
½ T Tabasco sauce
1 lb Medium shrimp,
    slightly cooked, peeled
    and deveined

Sauté onion and green pepper in butter in a large skillet until tender. Stir in flour, stirring constantly. Gradually add water and tomato sauce. Cook over medium heat until mixture is thickened. Stir in next 6 ingredients. Add shrimp. Cover. Reduce heat to low and let simmer for 10 minutes, stirring occasionally. Serve over rice.

Wine Suggestion: Robert Mondavi, White Zinfandel.

The Parlour Car

I F IT'S ROMANCE, RELAXATION AND EXQUISITE CUISINE you're looking for, why not experience these amenities in the privacy of your own elegant dining room? This is what The Parlour Car restaurant offers.

The Parlour Car is steeped in tradition. It's a beautifully restored 1887 railroad car that, ironically, sits on the original site of the Midland Railroad line that ran through Aspen. It was built by Pullman & Co. Originally, there were 80 private wooden cars built at that time. Today, eight/ten remain. In those days, railroads donated private cars to Presidents during their term of office. Theodore Roosevelt used these cars to tour Colorado on his many hunting trips to the Redstone Castle.

The Parlour Car was found in Welby, Colorado and carefully moved to Aspen. Owner Tim Terral found old Colorado Midland railroad ties and laid them down on this site so that The Parlour Car would appear authentic.

One year was spent restoring this wonderful old car. All the wood is original. It was soon to be decorated with the style and sentiment of the Victorian Age in mind. Unfortunately, because the wood had been painted white, it had to be stripped and brought back to its former elegance.

The Parlour Car has seven individual, private rooms, each decorated and furnished with a flair all its own. Many of the names reflect their original use—the bedroom, the study, the dining room, the porter's room, the galley, the Marquette and the Pullman. Newly added, for larger parties, is the Banquette Caboose with its own separate entrance and deck. Customers love the tiny, authentic water closets, complete with pull-chain toilets!

It's rather like visiting a museum. The ceiling, beyond the entrance, was hand painted. It took four devoted house painters from San Francisco 500 hours to paint the intricate design. There are wonderful pictures of trains and railroads on the walls, beautiful stained glass and lovely chandeliers.

A restaurant such as The Parlour Car could not survive in Aspen without fabulous food to complement its atmosphere. Each night they feature a different five-course meal. Terral describes the menu as "innovative French and American cuisine. We also refer to it as 'cross-over cuisine' to encompass the flavors of the Southwest and New Orleans."

Dining at The Parlour Car is an extraordinary experience. Terral invites you to "enjoy your ride into the past."

Boule de Niege

SERVES 12

8 oz Semi-sweet
   chocolate
½ C Strong coffee
½ C Butter
1 C Sugar
3 C Heavy cream
5 Eggs
Whipped cream

Melt the chocolate and coffee together. Stir in the butter and sugar alternately in small batches. Scald the heavy cream. Beat the eggs together in a large bowl. Pour scalded cream into eggs and whisk together. Then stir in the chocolate mixture. Pour this mixture into a heavy saucepan and stir constantly until very hot. Do not boil! Strain. Line the bottom of 12 ramekins with buttered parchment paper. Fill the ramekins. Bake in towel-lined baking pan filled with 150 degrees water at 325 degrees for 40 minutes (or until knife inserted comes out clean). Cool and cover. To serve, set the ramekins in warm water (until the mixture loosens). Use a spatula around sides, discard paper and place on a plate. Put whipped cream in a pastry bag and dot the chocolate mixture to resemble a snowball!

Shrimp à la Cluny

AN APPETIZER SERVING 12

2 lbs Shrimp, raw
weight, cooked, peeled
and deveined (save
peels) shrimp size, 21-
25
1 T Shallots, minced
3 T Butter
2 C Mushrooms, sliced
Pinch thyme
2 Bay leaves
Salt and pepper to taste
2 t Brandy
1 ¾ C White wine
1 ½ C Heavy cream
3 Egg yolks
1 T Parsley, minced
½ t Dry chervil
½ t Dry tarragon
1 t Lemon juice

Make shrimp stock: boil shrimp shells, 1 cup white wine, 1 cup cold water and 1 bay leaf for 10 minutes. Strain and reduce until it equals ½ cup. Sauté shallots in butter in a sauté pan for 1 minute. Add mushrooms, thyme, bay leaf, salt and pepper. Simmer for a few minutes to heat through. Raise the heat slightly, add brandy and flame it. Shake until the flame dies. Add ¾ cup warm white wine and the shrimp stock and simmer for about 1 minute. In a wide pan, reduce the pan juice by ⅔ (10 minutes or so). Combine the cream, yolks, herbs and stir carefully into the reduced pan sauce. Cook a few minutes to thicken slightly (slow flame). Add shrimp, lemon juice, salt and pepper to taste. Serve in scallop shell.

Wine Suggestion: Pouilly-Fumé De Ladoucette, 1983.

Stuffed Chicken Breasts

AN APPETIZER SERVING 8

2 Boneless, skinless
   chicken breasts
1 C Fine bread crumbs
½ C Flour
1 Egg
3 oz Chèvre
12 oz Sundried
   tomatoes
White wine
3 oz Prosciutto ham,
   thinly sliced
⅓ oz Fresh basil,
   chopped
¼ lb Fresh spinach,
   blanched

SAUCE
1 C Red wine vinegar
1 C Brown sugar
1 Onion, finely diced
1½ C Chicken stock
1 T Flour
1 T Butter
1 T Dijon mustard
1 T Whole-grain
   mustard

Soak sundried tomatoes in white wine (just enough to cover them) for 1 hour. Pound the chicken breasts, between cellophane, with a meat cleaver until it's ½ the thickness. Unfold the blanched spinach leaves and place on top of breasts. Then, place Prosciutto on top of spinach. Mix chèvre, basil and roughly chopped sundried tomatoes. Split this mixture in half. With your hands, make 2 cylindrical "logs" (diameter—the size of a nickel). Place the "logs", 1 on each breast (on top of the ham) approximately ¼ of the way from one end. Roll the chicken breast over the log, then roll again. Secure (on the underside) with toothpicks.

■ Lightly dust the breasts with flour, then coat with a beaten egg (add a bit of water to the egg). Roll lightly in bread crumbs. Lightly oil a thick sauté pan. Turn to medium heat. When hot, evenly brown the breasts (lightly). Place them on a small baking pan and bake in a preheated 375 degrees oven for 12 minutes. Remove and let sit for 3 minutes.

■ Make the sauce: in a saucepan, mix first 3 ingredients. Reduce by ½. Add chicken stock and simmer 5 minutes. In another pan, melt the butter and add the flour. Whisk together (to make a roux) and add to stock mixture. Simmer 5 minutes or until thickened. Strain. Add salt and white pepper to taste and the mustards. Then, slice chicken ¾", 16 slices (2 medallions per person). To serve, place the sauce on the plates, then the medallions on the sauce.

Wine Suggestion: Puligny-Montrachet, 1985 Joseph Drouhin.

Pinocchio's

WELL KNOWN FOR ITS DELICIOUS PIZZA, PINOCCHIO'S is a tradition in Aspen. Their pizza was recommended by the *New York Times. Skiing Magazine* wrote this praise, "Pinocchio's may well be the best pizza place in the country."

You may remember Pinocchio's when it was next to Crossroad Drugs. It was funky and laid-back. Then, they basically served sandwiches, salads and pizza. Owners Doug and Monica Hose felt a need to expand the menu and added more Italian items.

They moved across the way to their new location below Sabbatini's. Doug felt it was time for a change in Pinocchio's image. The restaurant is now contemporary. Glass blocks cemented together serve as dividers. Doug tells me, "The reason for the glass is to lighten up the restaurant. The glass reflects the light from outside to brighten up the inside."

In addition to their pizza, Pinocchio's serves homemade soups, salads of all kinds, unusual sandwiches, hamburgers, antipasti, desserts and their wonderful homemade Italian Hearth Bread.

Stracciatella Parmesan.

THIS IS A SOUP!

SERVES 8

12 C Chicken broth
1 C Parmesan cheese,
   grated
½ C Chablis wine
8 C Fresh spinach,
   chopped and packed
4 Eggs, beaten
Pinch white pepper and
   salt

Combine 10 cups chicken broth and chablis in a stock pot and bring to a boil. Whisk in spinach and eggs. Reduce heat to medium low and simmer until the eggs are cooked to a stringy consistency. Add grated Parmesan and 2 cups chicken broth (less broth if you'd like it thicker). Add salt and pepper to taste. Serve with an antipasti salad and bread.

Wine Suggestion: 1982 Sebastiani, Chardonnay.

Tortellini with Pesto and Cream.

Make chicken broth. Add tomatoes, carrots, cabbage, onion, celery and wine. Bring to a boil, then cook until carrots are half cooked. Add the tortellinis and spices. When the tortellinis are done (soft), add the pesto and cream. Bring to a boil once again. Serve and enjoy!

THIS IS A SOUP!

MAKES 1 GALLON

8 C Chicken broth
2 Fresh tomatoes, diced medium
2 Carrots, diced medium
1 ½ C Red cabbage, diced medium
1 Medium size onion, diced medium
2 Celery stalks, diced medium
3 T Fresh or store bought pesto sauce (recipe follows)
2 C Heavy cream
½ C White wine
1 lb Bag frozen tortellini noodles
Pinch white pepper
Pinch basil

Fresh Pesto Sauce

1 C Packed fresh basil leaves
¼ C Olive oil
2 T Pine nuts (found at specialty or health food stores)
½ C Fresh Parmesan
2 Cloves garlic

Combine all ingredients in blender and purée.

Wine Suggestion: Soave Bertani.

Poppies Bistro Café

"**W**E WANT TO PLEASE AND TITILLATE THE PALATE in a pleasing atmosphere with a touch of elegance." This is the goal of owners Michael Hull and Earl Jones. This charming Victorian restaurant located on the outskirts of Aspen, was formerly a residence and dates back to 1886. You immediately feel the charm of age upon entering Poppies. It has the atmosphere most people seek out when looking for a fine dining experience.

It's very romantic with original Franklin Halofain lamps hanging over each table. The wainscot wood panels on the walls tend to glow and give the dining room a warmer feel.

It's the little things about Poppies that will charm you. There's a different antique vase on each table and the fresh flowers vary. The pictures on the walls are fun and interesting. (Earl likes to move them around.) Lace curtains in the windows, wine bottles displayed around the dining room, tiny candles glowing and classical music are there to visually and sensually please you.

Chef Alan Mello serves creative classical cuisine with a contemporary flavor. Mello, who graduated from the Culinary Institute of America, has been the chef and kitchen manager since Poppies first opened. He has a reputation for cooking fresh seafood with wondrous sauces enhanced by fresh herbs and spices. Steak Au Poivre has been a favorite since the restaurant opened in 1981. Patrons appreciate their much-loved bread and their homemade sausages, patés and desserts.

Poppies has a basic menu with a "specials" sheet that changes each evening. This presents a challenge and allows Mello to be constantly creative. It keeps life interesting for this young chef who is always experimenting and traveling in order to learn more.

Poppies glows in the winter and comes to life in the summer. Live, brilliantly colored orange poppies sprout up by the entrance. Their green lawn and magnificent array of flowers, arranged in pots of all shapes and sizes, make for a perfect setting. Dining in their garden on a warm summer day is an experience not to be missed.

Poppies' Crab Wonton

SERVES 6

½ lb Blue lump crab
¼ Red pepper, finely diced
2 Cloves mashed garlic
2 T Shallot, finely diced
2 T Anaheim pepper, finely diced
¼ lb Butter
6 Wonton skins
Oil for deep frying

SAUCE
2 T Shallot, chopped
1 Large red holland bell pepper
1 ½ C Cream
Salt and pepper

Mix all ingredients except crab into room temperature butter. Divide crab and butter between the six wonton skins. See a Chinese cookbook for details on wonton rolling.

■ To make sauce: in a little butter over low heat, sweat pepper and shallot with salt and pepper until pepper is cooked well, all the way through. Add cream and reduce until slightly thick. Purée in blender and adjust seasoning.

■ For a neat presentation, do another sauce with yellow bell pepper. Put 2 sauces on a plate and swirl together slightly or put one down and draw a pattern on it with the other.

■ Deep fry wontons at 350 degrees until golden brown, 2-3 minutes. Serve on top of sauces with chopped chives.

Wine Suggestion: Louis Latour, Meursault.

Poppies' Halibut en Papillote

SERVES 6

Oil
Parchment paper
  (found at specialty
  stores)
6 6 oz Halibut fillets
2 Leeks, rinsed and
  chop ½" pieces
¾ C Mushrooms, sliced
½ Clove garlic
1 C Dry white wine
2 oz Sweet butter, room
  temperature
1 Small handful
  chopped fresh
  tarragon
1 Egg and 1 yolk
Salt and white pepper

In hot oil (enough to cover the bottom of the pan), with a small chip of butter thrown in at the last second, sauté mushrooms and minced garlic over high heat for 2 minutes. Season with salt and white pepper. Add chopped leeks and just enough wine to moisten. Sweat, covered over very low heat until leeks are opaque. Add remaining wine and reduce by ½. Swirl in butter to thicken. Do not stop stirring until butter is completely incorporated. Add fresh tarragon.

■ Lay halibut in a piece of heart shaped parchment paper twice the size of fish, season fish with salt and white pepper, cover with leek mixture. Brush edges of paper with beaten egg and starting at one end, do a tiny fold the whole way down, brush with egg again and fold again twice. Twist end for a sure seal. Brush parchment paper with vegetable oil and bake at 425 degrees for approximately 12-15 minutes or until fully blown up.

■ Serve in bag and cut at table.

Wine Suggestion: Chateau Montelena, Chardonnay.

Potato-Leek and Fennel Soup with Greens

SERVES 8

2 Quarts good chicken
   stock
2-3 Leeks, washed and
   roughly chopped
3 Small baking
   potatoes, cut 1" cubes
1 Bulb fresh fennel, cut
   1" cubes
1 Handful mixed stiff
   salad greens (endive,
   green kale, mustard
   greens, etc.)
½ C Crème fraiche
   (recipe follows)
2 T Oil
¼ C White wine
Salt, black pepper

CRÈME FRAICHE
1 pint Heavy cream
1 T Buttermilk

Two days in advance, make crème fraiche: add the buttermilk to the cream, mix well and cover. Let sit at room temperature for 2 days until thickened, then refrigerate.
■ Bring chicken stock to simmer gently over medium heat. In margarine or oil, gently sauté all ingredients except for greens. After 2 minutes, add a little white wine and sweat covered over very low heat, approximately 30 minutes until all veggies are opaque.
■ Add above mixture to stock along with the fresh greens and purée in a blender. Make sure the top is loose, so it doesn't blow up in your face. Add crème fraiche to the last batch in blender. Add salt and black pepper to taste.

The kicker: this is a hearty cold weather soup, a light meal with some good bread!

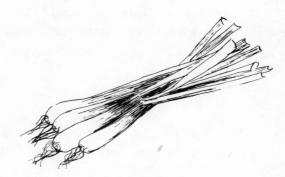

Poppycock's

REMEMBER THE LEMONS IN THE WINDOW? THEY ALWAYS caught my attention. Used to make fresh lemonade, the lemons also served as an eye catcher for anyone passing by. They lured you into Poppycock's, a tiny crêperie that also served cappucinos, health drinks, soups and home-baked desserts. From 1971-1986, it was located in the Brand Building. With only seven stools, you could always walk up to the outside window to order.

They were famous in Aspen for their spinach crêpes—large crêpes made-to-order with a thick, hearty spinach filling. Their dessert crêpes, four to choose from, were also popular.

Owners Josie and Mark Butzier had to move their tiny eatery in the summer of '86 when the Brand Building was renovated. They found their new home in the Aspen Square Building. Poppycock's is now a contemporary café with table service. They have retained a counter to satisfy customers who are in a hurry.

The original menu remained with the addition of breakfast and more lunch items. Breakfast includes: delicious french toast made from brioche and topped with fruit, five varieties of pancakes (customers adore their Macadamia Nut Oatmeal Pancakes) and four innovative egg dishes. Lunch now includes sandwiches on their homemade bread, a variety of lovely fresh salads with homemade dressings and three pasta meals (Linguine with Pesto, Pine Nuts and Fresh Goat Cheese is a favorite).

The new Poppycock's was an instant success. Word spread quickly of the fresh, wholesome and delicious food with grand specials that change daily.

Black Bean Chili

SERVES 6

¼ C Oil
1 Onion, chopped
¾ C Green pepper,
   diced
1 Red pepper, diced
1 ½ T Garlic, minced
2 T Paprika
½ t Cayenne
½ t Salt
2 Fresh Jalapeño
   peppers, chopped very
   small
2 C Black beans, cooked
1 ½ C Chopped tomato
   in purée
1 T Cumin seed
1 T Oregano
Sour cream
Grated cheddar cheese
Avocado

Sauté first 8 ingredients in oil until the onions are clear and translucent. Add black beans and tomato. Roast cumin seed and oregano until aromatic. Add to chili and cook slowly for an hour. If too thick, add water for desired consistency. Top with sour cream, cheddar cheese and a slice of avocado.

Pecan Pie

Mix pie crust ingredients well and press into pie pan or tart tin. Mix together pie filling ingredients and pour into unbaked pie shell. Bake at 350 degrees until set (about 45 minutes).

PIE CRUST
½ C Butter
1 Egg
1 ½ C Flour
¼ C Sugar
¼ t Salt

PIE FILLING
3 Eggs, beaten
1 C Brown sugar
⅓ C Butter, melted
1 C Dark corn syrup
1 C Pecans
1 t Brandy, rum or
vanilla

Veggie Pancakes with Crème Fraiche

Shred first 3 ingredients. Mix with next 6 ingredients. You may find you may need to add a bit more beaten egg and flour if it doesn't blend together well enough. Scoop out 2 tablespoons of mixture and fry at 350 degrees on a griddle or in a frying pan in a mixture of butter and oil until lightly brown. Flip and fry other side. Top with garnishes.

SERVES 2

1 Zucchini
1 Carrot
1 Potato
1 Egg, beaten
1/8 t Nutmeg
3 1/4 C Flour
4 t Garlic salt
1/2 t Pepper
1/4 C Cooked wild rice
1 T Butter
1 T Oil

GARNISH
Crème Fraiche or sour
   cream
Chives
Watercress

Wild Mushroom and Pistachio Strudel

Sauté mushrooms in butter. Mix next 4 ingredients and drain very well. Add cheese. Cool mixture and spread over 8" X 8" sheet of puff pastry. Roll like a jelly roll and place on ungreased sheet pan with sides. Brush top with beaten egg, crimp ends and bake at 400 degrees until puffed and brown (about 30 minutes).

APPETIZER OR SIDE DISH

¼ lb Wild mushrooms
1 lb Domestic
    mushrooms
½ C Butter, soft
½ t Pepper
3 T Dijon mustard
2 t Sherry
½ C Roasted pistachios
½ C Shredded Gruyère
    cheese
1 Egg
Puff pastry

The Red Onion

THE RED ONION'S CHARM COMES FROM ITS HISTORY. Still in its original location, the Red Onion is one of the few famous old mining-day saloons still operating. Tom Latta had "The Brick Saloon" built in 1892. The original fixtures and furnishings were elegant for their day. The club rooms, where billiards and pool were played, were praised as the "handsomest in the West," by the *Aspen Daily News*.

"Sporting men" of the region patronized The Brick Saloon. Their interests were prize-fighting, wrestling, cycling and other sporting events popular during that era. Today, pictures of prize-fighters on the walls serve as evidence of the past. A separate entrance led upstairs in case a man was in need of a "good time with a lady." A back door was provided for a discreet departure!

After World War II, Jonny Litchfield bought The Brick Saloon and changed its name to the Red Onion which means "something out of the ordinary." Skiing became Aspen's claim to fame, and with it, the Onion became the most popular bar in town for après-ski.

Werner Kuster purchased the Onion in 1953 and turned it into an internationally famous night club and restaurant.

The Red Onion is now owned by Dave (Wabs) Walbert and Bud Nicholson. Although a third smaller in size than it was, "Wabs" stresses, "It's still one of the oldest bars in town. We've kept it up through the years to look like it did in the 1800's. It has that great western flavor."

Look around at the historic old photographs on the walls of the Smuggler Mine, old Victorian homes and the Onion as it was in 1948, surrounded by empty lots and looking a bit lonesome.

The food the Onion now serves is Mexican and "good old" American. In the summer, outdoor patio dining is provided for your enjoyment!

Chiles Rellenos

SERVES 4

8 Fresh Anaheim chiles-
should be smooth (not
wrinkled with age)
1 Lb Monterey Jack
cheese
Oil for deep frying

BATTER
1 ½ C Flour
1 t Baking powder
½ t Salt
¼ t Pepper
1 ½ C Milk
2 Eggs, separated

SAUCE
1 Onion, medium,
halved and sliced
2 Cloves garlic, minced
2 T Olive oil
1 14 ½ Oz Can chicken
broth
2 C Whole peeled
tomatoes, coarsely
diced with liquid

1 Small can diced
chiles, (Ortega)
1 C Raw diced chicken
meat
Salt and pepper

Roast the chiles over a gas flame or in the broiler until well charred on all sides. Place the chiles in a paper bag and let sweat for 10 minutes. Carefully peel; make a lengthwise slit in the side of each chile, rinse under cold water to remove seeds and pat dry. Cut the cheese into ½ " by ½ " strips, 4-5" long. Insert the cheese into each chile and overlap the flap on the chiles to seal.

■ Sift all the dry batter ingredients together. Add the milk and egg yolks and beat to combine. Whip the egg whites to soft peaks and fold them into the batter carefully.

■ To make the sauce: sauté the onions in oil until transparent. Add the garlic and cook 1 minute longer. Add the remaining ingredients and simmer for 45 minutes. Roll the stuffed chiles in flour, then dip them in the batter and deep fry them in 360 degree oil until golden brown. Drain and keep the chiles in a 300 degrees oven until the remaining ones are fried. Ladle the sauce over the chiles and serve immediately.

The Sardy House

THIS NEWLY RENOVATED BRICK VICTORIAN HOUSE ON Main Street is now a hotel. But it's more than that; it's quiet, it's homey, the rooms are individually decorated, the views are magnificent, elegant dinners are served and the staff is friendly. It rather reminds me of one of those wonderful guest houses on the Island of Nantucket, filled with nostalgia and romance. The Sardy House also reminds me of Aspen as it was in the 1800's.

Originally built in 1895, it housed two families before Tom and Alice Rachel Sardy took up residence.

The parlour is very Victorian and lends itself to reading and relaxation. The dining room is beyond the parlour.

The public is invited to dine at The Sardy House for breakfast, brunch and dinner. You'll experience the splendor of eating in a country inn-type atmosphere. It's small and intimate, with fresh flowers on the tables. Classical music plays in the background. This lovely room is enhanced by bay windows that bring in light.

The breakfast menu allows you to choose from a special each morning: brie omelettes, fruit bread, french toast made with their homemade cinnamon-raisin bread or oatmeal molasses waffles. Freshly brewed coffee adds just the right touch. Sunday brunch is an extension of breakfast with the addition of a cold sliced chicken breast served with homemade tarragon mayonnaise, shrimp pasta with snow peas and a filet mignon sandwich.

Chef Robert Wieser, a native of Aspen, designed the menu which he describes as "French nouvelle cuisine in the Victorian style." With only a few specialized items, Wieser concentrates on dazzling his customers with superb creations.

Their dinners invite romance. For a special evening, The Sardy House is an experience you'll long remember.

Apple-Brie Cheese Omelette

½ Apple, peeled, cored
   and thinly sliced
2 ½ T Butter
Dash of cinnamon,
   nutmeg, brown
   sugar, ginger
2 Eggs, room
   temperature
2 t Cream or milk
Dash of salt and pepper
2 T Diced Brie cheese

In a small pan, sauté apples in 1 tablespoon butter. Add a dash of cinnamon, nutmeg, ginger and brown sugar. Beat together eggs, cream or milk and a dash of salt and pepper just until blended. Melt remaining butter in omelette pan over high heat. Pour in egg mixture and prepare omelette. When it is set on bottom, fill with Brie cheese cubes. Fold or roll and slide out of pan onto warm plate. Arrange sautéed apple slices on top. Serve with orange pecan bread.

Orange Pecan Bread

Cream the butter, add sugar gradually. Beat with mixer until light. Beat in egg yolks one at a time. Add the grated orange rind. Grate only the orange zest. Sift flour, baking powder, soda and salt. Add dry mixture to the batter alternating with ½ cup orange juice beginning and ending with flour mixture. Gently fold in pecans. Beat the whites until stiff and fold them carefully into batter. Bake at 350 degrees for 50-60 minutes in a 8 ½" x 4 ½" greased pan. Make the glaze: combine orange juice and sugar. Simmer gently for 5 minutes until it thickens. Pour over hot bread.

BREAD
1 Stick softened butter
¾ C Granulated sugar
2 Eggs, separated
1 Grated orange rind
1 ½ C All purpose flour
1 ½ t Baking powder
¼ t Baking soda
Pinch of salt
½ C Fresh orange juice
1 C Chopped pecans

GLAZE
½ C Fresh orange juice
½ C Sugar

Stuffed Chicken Normandy

SERVES 4

STUFFING
½ C Minced onion
½ Stick butter
2 Golden delicious apples, peeled and chopped
2 t Fresh sage
2 t Fresh thyme
2 t Lemon juice
4 Chicken breasts, boned and skinned

DREDGING
2 Large eggs
2 t Water
½ C Bread crumbs
½ C Salted chopped cashews
¼ C Vegetable oil

Stuffing: cook onion in butter until soft; add apples, sage and thyme. Salt and pepper to taste, sauté for 10 minutes. Stir in lemon juice and cool the mixture. Lay out breasts, lightly pounded. Put 2 tablespoons of filling on one side of the breast and fold over the other half. Fasten the edges with toothpicks. Lightly dredge in flour, then egg, then cashews and bread crumb mixture. Let chill for 1 hour to hold shape. In a heavy skillet, heat the oil to brown the breasts. Transfer to a baking dish and bake 20-25 minutes at 350 degrees. Make the sauce while breasts are cooking. Pour fat from skillet, add onion, wine and the cider. Boil until liquid is evaporated. Add the stock and reduce by half. Add the cream and Calvados until thickened.

Wine Suggestion: Valfleur, Alexander, Chardonnay 1983.

SAUCE
½ C Minced onion
¾ C Dry white wine
¾ C Apple cider
1 C Chicken stock
1 C Heavy cream
4 T Calvados Apple Brandy

Stuffed Tiger Prawns Florentine

AN APPETIZER SERVING 6

¼ C Minced garlic
¼ C Minced onion
¼ C Minced shallots
12 Tiger Prawns
Salt and pepper
¼ C Dry white wine
2 C Spinach, chopped
Butter
¼ C Parmesan cheese
¼ C Chopped nuts (we
   use almonds)
¼ C Bread crumbs,
   seasoned

To make the stuffing, sauté the garlic, onion and shallots. Add the spinach, white wine and salt and pepper to taste. Clean the shrimp, and with the shell on, cut through the shrimp without breaking the shell and devein. Place in a heat-proof baking dish with tails up. Stuff shrimp. Add a little white wine and butter for baking. Mix together the Parmesan, chopped nuts and the bread crumbs. Sprinkle mixture (dry) over shrimp and bake at 350 degrees until prawns turn bright orange and separate from the shell. Serve immediately.

Wine Suggestion: Meursault, Jaboulet-Vercherre 1985.

Sea Grill and Oyster Bar at The Copper Kettle

THE ORIGINAL RESTAURANT, THE COPPER KETTLE, WAS established by retired U.S. Foreign Service officers Sara and Army Armstrong in 1954. The Armstrongs collected recipes on their travels around the world. This became the premise for their restaurant—to feature a different international menu each evening. They had such a multitude of recipes, that they amazed their customers by never repeating a dish. They served a seven-course meal in elegant surroundings.

Sirous Saghatoleslami took over ownership in 1973 and ran it in the same style for twelve years. During that period of time, Sirous discovered a discontentment amongst his guests. People were becoming more health conscious and wanted to eat lighter meals. In order to satisfy his clientele, he completely changed his concept. The menu changed along with a new name and a fresh new image.

Devotees are pleased to find a large menu featuring many varieties of fresh fish. Favorites include bouillabaisse, rack of lamb, New York strip steak and daily specials. The Oyster Bar serves oyster stew, clams, shrimp, mussels and Cajun specialties.

The Tippler Bar, upstairs, is one of Aspen's "in" spots. Conveniently located next to the Silver Queen Gondola, skiers meet for après-ski in its comfortable confines. Lunch, on its sunny deck or in their atrium, features the ever-popular Tapas bar. After dark, The Tippler comes alive with music, a large dance floor and a spectacular light show.

Cold Banana Soup

MAKES 12 SIX OUNCE SERVINGS

5 Medium-size
   bananas
1 Gallon apple cider
4 Whole cinnamon
   sticks
10-15 Whole cloves
1 T All-spice
½ C Sugar
1 Pint heavy cream
¼ C Banana Liqueur

Bring cider to a boil with the 3 spices. Reduce mixture by ⅔'s. Strain and cool. Peel and place the bananas in a large mixing bowl. Put in sugar and purée with a large fork. Don't get the mixture too smooth, leave small pieces of banana. Slowly stir in cider mixture, heavy cream and liqueur. Chill 2 hours before serving.

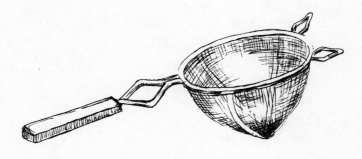

Shrimp Grand Marnier

SERVES 2

12 16-20 count
    Shrimp, shelled and
    deveined
¼ Green pepper, cut in
    julienne strips
¼ Red pepper, cut in
    julienne strips
1 Small carrot, cut in
    julienne strips
1 Small yellow squash,
    cut in julienne strips
10 Pieces of orange
    sections, remove skins
5 T Butter
½ C Grand Marnier
6 T Cold Butter

Place 5 tablespoons butter in medium-sized sauté pan on medium-high heat. Put shrimp in pan and cook one side. Turn shrimp over, put in vegetable strips, orange sections and Grand Marnier. Let liquid reduce by ⅔'s. Mix in the cold butter and remove from heat.

The kicker: this is a quick and easy dish and is wonderful served over rice pilaf.

Wine Suggestion: Chimney Rock, 'Napa Valley', Chardonnay.

Shlomo's Deli

WHEN SHLOMO BEN-HAMOO MOVED TO ASPEN eight years ago from Israel, he saw a definite need for an authentic New York-style delicatessen. Having fallen in love with this area and knowing Aspen was the place he wanted to stay and raise a family, he set out to make this vision a reality. He went to New York City, the source, to study deli operations and to gain contacts for food distributors.

He found a perfect location in the Little Nell's Building at the base of Aspen Mountain. Shlomo's Deli became an immediate success. It's where the skiers meet in the mornings for a hearty breakfast before heading up the gondola for a day of skiing.

The atmosphere is casual. Choose from a booth or their horseshoe counter. It has the flavor of a diner with jukeboxes and friendly, fast-moving waitresses.

The food is exactly what you'd expect. Huge corned beef and pastrami sandwiches, reubens, kosher salami (blessed by Rabbi Goldman and Rabbi Leff) and lox and bagels are examples of Shlomo's fare. Their famous chicken soup, with an enormous matzo ball, has cured many a case of Aspen's flu. They are also known for serving the best milk shakes in town. Summer or winter, you'll find bikers and skiers sitting at the counter devouring a thick, delicious milk shake after a hard day's workout!

Shlomo, incredible as it may seem, is always there to greet you, making you feel at home (he speaks four languages) and making sure your meal was satisfactory. Tourists are always asking him to move to their hometown to open a deli. It's the ultimate compliment. Shlomo told me, "This place proves that you don't have to be Jewish to eat deli food! We get people from all walks of life and they all enjoy it here."

Shlomo, with his cheerfulness and sincere congeniality, complements Aspen. He reminds us that Aspen is still a town, and not just a glittery resort.

Chocolate Cake

THIS MAKES A VERY LARGE
CAKE AND USES TWO 10" X
2" SPRINGFORM PANS.

4 C Flour
4 oz Hershey's breakfast
   cocoa
1 t Baking soda
1 ¾ t Baking powder
1 t Salt
2 ½ C Sugar
4 Eggs
8 oz Melted butter
1 t Vanilla

FROSTING
1 ½ 16 ounce boxes
   Powdered sugar
1 t Vanilla
4 oz Hershey's breakfast
   cocoa
4 oz Melted butter
5-6 oz Milk

In one mixing bowl, add first 5 ingredients and mix well. In another bowl, add next 4 ingredients and mix well. Add the first bowl to the second bowl, then add 4 cups cold water and mix well. Pour into two pre-greased 10" X 2" cake pans and bake at 350 degrees for 65 minutes.

■ To make frosting: mix first 4 ingredients well in mixer or Cuisinart. Add milk slowly until desired consistency is obtained.

Smuggler Land Office

TIM COTTRELL IS THE PROUD OWNER OF THIS NEWLY renovated restaurant and bar. Its atmosphere takes you back to before the turn of the century when the Smuggler Mining Company was in operation. The actual Smuggler Mining Company office opened in July of 1879, and by 1888 was shipping 25 tons of silver ore per day to the smelter! As history goes, with the devaluation of silver, many of the mines in Aspen closed. The Smuggler Mining Company continued to operate, and in 1894, saw its success—the largest nugget of silver ever mined, 90% pure, and weighing almost one ton.

If you visited Aspen in the 70's, you'll remember the Smuggler Land Office to have been the Sub Shoppe, also owned by Cottrell. Now, after an intense restoration, the result is an elegant, three-leveled restaurant complete with stained glass, original U.S. Geographic Survey maps from the 1890's (of Smuggler and Aspen Mountains) and the two original vaults that have been beautifully repainted.

To complement this decor, Cottrell serves gourmet Cajun and Creole food. The credit goes to his chef, Peter Soto who trained with the famous Paul Prudhomme in Denver. The Smuggler uses their own spice mixtures. Herbs grown in their garden are also used in cooking.

Their specialties include: Blackened Redfish or Salmon, Cajun Broiled Shrimp, Blackened New York Steak or Cajun Seafood Gumbo.

Summer lends itself to dining outdoors in their garden café. What could be nicer than listening to a quartet from the Aspen Music School play jazz while sampling the Smuggler's Cajun or Creole cooking?

Striving to be unique, Cottrell has the only wine bar in town. Customers can purchase vintage California and French wines by the glass, rather than ordering an entire bottle. This wine bar is run on a nitrogen-displacement system.

Cottrell has received the ultimate compliment from a Southern guest, "That's as good as my gumbo!"

Creole Sauce

In a saucepan, brown the garlic in the butter. Add the vegetables and clove and sauté until tender. Add the liquids and simmer until reduced by ⅓.

1 C each and diced-red and green peppers, yellow onion and celery
1 T Garlic purée
1 Whole clove
1 T Lemon juice
¾ C Red wine (i.e. Louis Latour 1984, Beaujolais-Villages)
½ C Butter
1 6 ounce Can diced tomatoes in purée

Perfect for seafood and beef.

Remoulade Sauce

Combine all ingredients in a mixing bowl and refrigerate. Serve cold over shrimp, crab, hamburgers, etc.

1 C Mayonnaise
1 oz Chili sauce
1 oz Hot horseradish
1 t Red wine vinegar
½ C Celery, chopped small
½ C Scallions, chopped small

1 t each: Dry mustard, thyme, chili powder, garlic salt, onion salt, paprika and basil
1 T Prepared mustard
2 Dashes Tabasco sauce

Oysters Elysee

SERVES 4

1 t Thyme leaves
1 Bay leaf
2 Pinches nutmeg
½ t White pepper
Pinch salt
1 6 ounce can clam
   juice
2 C Heavy cream
White roux
1 ½ C Grated Swiss
   cheese
Dash Tabasco
2 oz White wine
Squeeze lemon juice
4 Dozen fresh, shucked
   oysters and juice
1 lb Spinach, cleaned

To make the white sauce: in a saucepan, add the first 7 ingredients and bring to a boil. Then simmer for 20 minutes. You can thicken to a medium consistency with a white roux if needed. In another saucepan, bring 2 cups of the white sauce, white wine, Tabasco and lemon juice to a gentle boil. Whisk the cheese (save a bit for later) into the fluids until it becomes even. Add oysters and simmer covered for 5 minutes.

■ Take the oysters out of the pan and place them in individual baking dishes lined with the spinach. Cover with the sauce and top with remaining cheese. Brown the tops of the dishes in a broiler and serve.

Wine Suggestion: McDowell Fumé Blanc, 1984.

Red Beans and Rice

SERVES 6-8

1 lb Dried red beans
1 Ham bone
1 ½ Medium onions
1 lb Andouille sausage,
    diced
½ lb Smoked ham, diced
1 C Green onion, sliced
Salt, cayenne and
    paprika to taste
3 C Rice, cooked

Soak beans in salt water for 12-24 hours. In a large pot, place beans in water (enough to cover beans by ½). Boil for 1 ½ hours and add water if needed. Add ham bone and boil 1 more hour. In a sauté pan, place chopped onions and Andouille sausage and sauté until onions are clear. Remove ham bone. Add onions and sausage and simmer for 1 hour. Add ham and seasonings, and simmer ½ hour or until gravy thickness. Serve over cooked rice and garnish with green onions on top.

Wine Suggestion: Preston Zinfandel, 1983.

The Steak Pit

ORIGINALLY, IN THE EARLY 60'S, THE STEAK PIT operated out of the Cooper St. Pier Building downstairs. The owners, Peter and Barbara Guy, came out from the East expecting to be in Aspen for a year and decided to stay. They say it was a combination of the feel of a small town, the mountains, the weather and more importantly, the people. "Back then, there wasn't a lot going on and there were very few restaurants."

The Steak Pit's original menu was small, offering mostly grilled steaks and beef kabobs. In 1968, they moved to the City Market Building and expanded their menu to include: Prime Rib, Teriyaki Chicken and Pork Chops, Australian Lobster Tails, Alaskan King Crab Legs and fresh fish.

They have the distinction of introducing the first salad bar on this continent. One of their waiters was from Hawaii (where the salad bar concept originated) and suggested trying it. Customers loved the idea of creating their own salads from a variety of fresh ingredients.

Barbara, better known as "Mom," makes a hot fudge sauce you could die for! Many patrons become addicted to her sundaes. "Mom's" Mocha Pie and Cheese Cake are also available.

The decor is Spanish/Mexican and the atmosphere is very relaxed. If you've ever been to The Steak Pit, you'll remember their large candle by the entrance. It was purchased at a pawn shop in Mexico City and has become quite a conversation piece—customers love it. The candle continues to grow by the year.

Cream of Spinach Soup

SERVES 14

7 oz Butter
1 Bunch green onions, chopped
4 10 oz packages chopped frozen spinach, thawed
1 ¾ quarts (60 oz) Homemade chicken stock or canned Swansons
½ C Flour
3 Egg yolks
1 C Heavy cream
¼ t Salt
¼ t White pepper
¾ t Nutmeg
Dash Tabasco

In a saucepan, melt 1 ounce butter. Add onions and sauté until soft. Add spinach with liquid and ½ cup water and simmer until just barely cooked. Cover while cooking. In a large pot, melt 6 ounces butter. Blend in flour and cook over low heat for 3-4 minutes. Do not let roux brown. Pour in chicken broth, stirring constantly with a wire whisk to blend. Cook until thickened (stirring often with whisk) and perfectly smooth. Add cooked spinach and green onions and simmer for 10 minutes.

■ Meanwhile, blend the egg yolks and heavy cream together until smooth and combined. Gradually add this to the hot soup, stirring constantly to blend. Season with spices.

The kicker: this soup freezes well. It may be prepared in advance, refrigerated and reheated over low heat, stirring occasionally.

Green Chile with Chicken Soup

SERVES 12

In a stock pot, melt butter. Add the onions and sauté until soft. Add green chiles and cook a few minutes more. Add chicken stock and meat and bring to a slow boil and simmer for 15-20 minutes.

■ Mix cornstarch with cold water and add to hot soup—stirring slowly until thickened. Gradually stir in Half & Half. Season to taste. Add 1-2 tablespoons of good chicken base if you desire more chicken flavor. Do not freeze.

¼ C Butter
4 Green onions, chopped
2 7-oz Cans diced green chiles
¾ lb Diced chicken meat, cooked

2 quarts Homemade chicken stock or canned Swansons
⅔ C Cornstarch
2 C Water
1 C Half & Half
White pepper

Lemon Ice

MAKES 1 1/2 QUARTS

Boil sugar and water for 5 minutes, add lemon juice and rind. Cool and freeze. I use a 5 quart ice cream freezer, but any will work. Check your instruction manual for ices and follow directions for freezing. I serve this with a teaspoon of rum poured over each serving.

4 C Water
2 C Sugar
¾ C Lemon juice
1 T Lemon rind, grated

Takah Sushi

THE *NEW YORK TIMES* STATES SIMPLY, "SOME OF THE best Japanese food between Manhattan and Malibu." Takah Sushi originated seven years ago and was Aspen's first Japanese restaurant. Owner Casey Coffman explains, "Japanese sushi bars and restaurants were very popular on the West Coast. Takah Sushi was the result of the feeling that Aspen needed something different. We took a chance." Locals and visitors alike are glad they did!

The restaurant is a combination of a sushi bar and a dining room that serves Japanese entrées. This appeals to non-sushi lovers.

Sushi, contrary to most people's belief, is not raw fish. Rather it is described as, "carefully prepared vinegared rice with something on top, most frequently raw, marinated or smoked fish or shellfish." California rolls, for example, contain no fish at all. The rice used is very difficult to make in order to achieve precisely the correct moisture content. It has a natural sweetness. Their sushi bar has mostly traditional items with some specials of their own. Casey boasts, "My Japanese chefs are perfectionists. Because of their techniques, our sushi bar has an exceptional level of quality." The sushi bar chefs dazzle you with their expertise and outstanding creations. It's a show worth watching with delicious results.

Sashimi, on the other hand, is something sliced and served without rice. The Japanese consider this to be one of the wonders of culinary delights. Casey told me, "The food has to be cut absolutely perfectly. If it's raw fish, it must be tender, tasty and very fresh. It must be the best!" Sashimi is always served with a garnish of daikon (a Japanese radish).

This whole concept of the Japanese style of presentation is much like their tea ceremonies—very simple and yet complex. They consider the look of the food to be just as important as how it tastes. Color, texture and design are combined to please you thoroughly.

If sushi is not to your liking, they also offer full course Japanese dinners in the dining room. Favorites include: chicken, steak and salmon teriyaki, vegetable tempura and crispy duck.

Tanoshi Hitotokio!

Naku Hivari

JAPANESE-STYLE FRIED
CHICKEN. AN APPETIZER
SERVING 6.

15-20 Chicken wings

MARINADE
2 C Soy sauce
*1 t Shichimi (Japanese
    7-spice powder)*
*Pinch fresh garlic,
    minced*
*½ t Fresh ginger,
    minced*
*¼ Of an orange,
    squeezed*
*Rice starch or
    cornstarch*
Oil for deep frying

Mix marinade ingredients together with chicken wings. Allow to sit at room temperature for 15-20 minutes. Dredge with rice starch or cornstarch. Deep fry in very hot oil for 1 ½-2 minutes. Arrange on lettuce leaves and serve with lemon slices.

Beverage Suggestion: Kirin or Sapporo—Japanese beer!

Summertime Soft Shell Crabs

AN APPETIZER SERVING 6

12 Soft shell crabs
Flour
Oil
Bibb lettuce
Daikon (Chinese white
    radishes)

SAUCE
2 C Rice vinegar
¾ C Sugar
1 Chili, very hot

Dredge crabs in flour and deep fry in hot oil for 2 minutes. Drain. Cut crabs in half (lengthwise) and arrange on lettuce. Garnish with shredded daikon. To make sauce: mix ingredients together and simmer for 5 minutes. Serve in a small dish when room temperature. Wrap a piece of crab in the lettuce with a small amount of daikon, dip in sauce and enjoy!

Wine Suggestion: Vouvray, Wildman.

Toros in Aspen

MEXICAN RESTAURANTS ARE EVER SO POPULAR. THE Aspen area has five. But the original Mexican restaurant is Toros. It's been in the same location next to Aspen Drug for 22 years, and that says a lot.

Steve Gray, the present owner, started working at Toros as a dishwasher. He came to Aspen as a ski bum and decided to stay. He eventually bought Toros and has since opened a branch in Minnetonka, Minnesota.

Toros has been recognized as having the best fajitas in Aspen. A fajita is an enchilada you create with a variety of fillings. Their tamales are made from scratch and come from an old New Mexican recipe that was handed down from the cook's grandmother. They offer three different varieties of tamales that are all cooked in corn husks.

Probably their most popular items are the chimichangas, the burritos, Toros' bean dip and Nacho Grande. Unlike most restaurants, they use a mixture of Monterey Jack and mild aged cheddar cheeses.

All the food is fresh and homemade daily. The recipes are all original and the food is consistent. And they definitely don't skimp on the portions!

To complement your meal, try one of their fabulous margaritas or choose from a large variety of Mexican beers.

The atmosphere is homey, relaxed and casual. The bar and seating area near the fireplace make Toros a great meeting place. You'll feel welcome to drink cocktails and snack on guacamole or to eat in the main dining room. The photographs on the walls were done exclusively for Toros by world renowned photographer, Paul Chesley. They help to create a warm, south-of-the-border feel.

Chili Con Queso

THIS IS A CHEESE SAUCE
WHICH CAN BE USED AS A
DIP OR AS A TOPPING ON
DIFFERENT ENTRÉES.

4 oz Lightly salted
  butter
3 ¼ lb Cheddar cheese
  sauce, aged and mild
3 Large green chili
  strips, mild, finely
  diced
2 Medium red
  tomatoes, cored, finely
  diced
4 oz Piquante sauce
12 oz Cream cheese

Combine and heat in a double boiler the butter, cheese sauce and cream cheese. Bring to a light bubble. Stir in chili strips, tomatoes and piquante sauce. Let simmer, stirring occasionally for 15-20 minutes, then serve.

Perfect Margarita

Combine Tequila, Cointreau and lime juice into mixing cup, shake or blend. Pour over ice into salt rimmed glass. Float Grand Marnier on top and serve with lime wedges if desired.

MAKES 1 MARGARITA

1 ½ oz Cuervo Especial
   Gold Tequila
¾ oz Cointreau liqueur
3 oz Sweet sour mix or
   Roses Lime Juice
½ oz Grand Marnier
   liqueur

Ute City Banque

THE UTE CITY BANQUE IS A BEAUTIFULLY APPOINTED bar and restaurant. It is named for the town of Aspen which was previously called Ute City.

This classic red brick building was erected in 1880 and was an operating bank from 1890-1963. Owner David Michael maintained the look with authentic teller windows and the original Victorian vault that sits behind the bar.

It's one of locals' and visitors' favorite restaurants—it has the Aspen feel. Plants, stained glass, a large oak bar, fans and windows that open to the Aspen scene all help to create a relaxed atmosphere. The bar is the hub of the downtown social scene. It's a wonderful place to meet friends and has a mix of Rugby players, locals with cowboy hats and couples dressed in their finest. They all seem to blend together and exchange conversation!

"The Ute's" menu combines regional and new cuisine with old favorites. Head chef David Zumwinkle (D.Z.) serves fresh fish, steaks, lamb, veal chops and pasta. Old favorites include rack of lamb, roast duckling and their famous spinach and cheese casserole (served at lunch). The menu also offers an interesting mix of Mexican, Cajun and French items.

Manager John Walla notes, "The idea behind our menu is to have something for everyone. We abandoned the recent fad of serving minuscule portions. We feel people in Aspen are active and want a decent amount of food. We serve gourmet food in a non-snobbish atmosphere. Our service is unpretentious. Our waiters can adapt to a customer's preference. They can be formal or low-key."

Walla is proud of their wine list, which is one of the largest in town. Their philosophy is that wine should be drunk first and talked about later. They offer very affordable wines and a large captain's list for older vintage wines.

After skiing or after a concert, you'll often hear, "Meet you at The Ute." It's just that kind of place.

Black Forest Crêpes

SERVES 8

BATTER
1 C Flour
1 C Milk
4 Eggs
Pinch salt
2 T Cocoa powder

FILLING
½ C Dark sweet pitted
   cherries
3 C Vanilla ice cream
1 T Peter Herring
   (cherry liqueur)
1 oz Shaved semi-sweet
   chocolate

HOT FUDGE SAUCE
1 oz unsweetened
   chocolate
1 oz Butter
¾ C Sugar
4 T Half and half
¼ t Vanilla

Mix batter ingredients together and let sit for 1 hour at room temperature. Make crêpes (see Maurice's Crêpes Suzette, page 72).Combine filling ingredients in a mixer. Do not let the ice cream melt. Freeze for at least 2 hours. To make the sauce, melt the chocolate and butter over low heat. Add and bring to a boil the sugar, half and half and vanilla. Simmer for 5 minutes. Fill crêpes, roll with ice cream filling and top with hot fudge sauce.

Fettuccine with Goat Cheese

SERVES 6

½ lb Broccoli flowerets
1 T Extra virgin olive oil
¾ C Chicken broth
1 t Fresh thyme leaves
3 T Unsalted butter
4 oz Goat cheese
Pinch salt
12 oz Fettuccine noodles, cooked al dente (we make our own)
1 T Toasted pine nuts

Sauté the broccoli in oil for 1 minute. Add the next 5 ingredients and boil until the cheese melts. Divide the noodles amongst 6 warm plates, add the sauce and top with pine nuts.

Wine Suggestion: Santa Margherita, Pinot Grigio.

Fruit Salad with Avocado Dressing

In a food processor, process first 7 ingredients until creamy. On 8 chilled plates, alternate slices of fruit and drizzle dressing over them. Garnish with freshly grated coconut if desired. Any fruit of your choice can be substituted.

Wine Suggestion: Chateau Potelle, Sauvignon Blanc, 'Napa Valley'.

SERVES 8

1 Avocado
2 T Lemon juice
½ t Salt
½ C Orange juice
2 T Honey
½ C Mayonnaise
Dash Tabasco
1 Cantaloupe
1 Honeydew melon
1 Papaya
2 Pears
1 C Strawberries

Spicy Grilled Shrimp

SERVES 6

1 C Salad oil
2 T Sesame oil
Zest of 1 orange
3 T Crushed red pepper
   flakes
4 t Chinese salted black
   beans (found at
   specialty or Chinese
   markets)
1 Clove garlic, peeled
   and crushed
30 Large shrimp, peeled
   and deveined

Heat both oils to 250 degrees. Remove from heat and add the next 4 ingredients. Store in a glass container and allow to sit overnight. Marinate the shrimp for 15 minutes and grill over hot coals until tender.

Wine Suggestion: Cardinal Richard Muscadet, 'Loire Valley'.

Chez Grandmère

A DREAM COME TRUE.

That's what Chez Grandmère is to Ruth and Bob Kevan. It all began when they retired and moved from Washington D.C. to Snowmass in 1972, with absolutely no experience in the food business. But, they had a strong vision.

It was not until after they had started and operated The Stew Pot, The Wineskin, The Upstairs Place and The Pepper Mill, that Chez Grandmère was born. It first opened in the space occupied by the Peppermill on the Snowmass Mall. After much planning by the Kevans, the format was finalized—a prix fixe, four-course dinner menu with only one seating each evening. It's a concept unique to any restaurant in Aspen or Snowmass.

The Kevan's guests love the freedom of choosing their own arrival time (between the hours of six and nine o'clock). This ensures a leisurely and relaxed dining experience with plenty of time for that extra cup of coffee and liqueurs.

After two years on the Mall, the Kevans had an opportunity to restore the old, small Victorian-style Hoagland ranch farmhouse by the Snowmass Center. The old house is constructed of logs covered with narrow siding, which was the style in those days. The Kevans left a small section of the logs exposed so that their visitors can see the original method of construction. The farmhouse was built sometime between 1903 and 1905.

An addition was built to accommodate seven tables. The same dining format was retained. The four-course dinner includes an apéritif with hors d'oeuvres; a fresh green salad with a homemade dressing which changes on a regular basis; fresh baked French bread; a choice among three entrées, always a fresh meat, a fowl and a fresh fish served with three fresh vegetables; and a wide selection from a Continental-style dessert cart. All of the desserts are baked on the premises.

The Executive Chef is Michel Poumay, a professionally trained Belgian. Michel is now a partner with the Kevans and serves as the general manager in addition to running the kitchen. Fiona Smollen is the Pastry Chef. She's a self-taught young Australian lady whose desserts are admired as much as Michel's masterpieces.

Brittany Almond Cake

FILLING
²/₃ C Almonds,
    preferably with skins
    on (for more flavor)
½ C Sugar
Egg white, enough to
    make a spreadable
    paste

CAKE
8 oz Butter
1 Whole egg
1 Extra yolk
½ C Sugar
2 t Orange flower
    water
¼ t Almond extract
1 ½ C Sifted flour
2 T Sifted cornstarch
⅓ t Baking powder
Pinch salt
⅓ C Ground almonds

Preheat oven to 350 degrees. Grease an 8 ½" springform pan. Grind almonds in food processor. Add sugar, a little egg white and water if necessary. Set filling aside. Cream butter well. Add egg and ⅔ of the extra yolk. Set the remainder aside in a small bowl with a teaspoon of water to use as a glaze. Add sugar and flavorings to cake batter and beat very well. Add dry ingredients. Turn half batter into cake pan. Cover with almond filling, then top with remaining batter. Beat glaze ingredients together with a fork. Paint top of cake lightly with glaze then make a crosshatch design in glaze with tines of fork. Bake for 30-35 minutes until firm and golden. Serve warm, with fresh crushed berries and heavy pouring cream.

This is an adaptation of a Madeleine Kamman recipe for a traditional cake made in Brittany. It is more suitable for preparing at home rather than in a restaurant because you can put it in the oven while you eat your dinner, then eat it at its best—warm and tender and aromatic, covered with crushed raspberries and a little heavy cream (not whipped).

Ilona Torte

CAKE
⅔ C Sugar
¼ C Coffee
6 oz Semi-sweet
  chocolate, chopped
1 t Vanilla
3 oz Butter
8 Eggs, separated
8 oz Hazelnuts, roasted
  and ground
Pinch salt

FROSTING
6 oz Semi-sweet
  chocolate, chopped
⅓ C Coffee
9 oz Butter
3 Egg yolks
½ C Confectioners'
  sugar
Frangelico (optional)

Preheat oven to 350 degrees. Grease two 9" round pans. Combine sugar and coffee in small saucepan and simmer until sugar is dissolved. Add chocolate and let it melt, stirring occasionally. Cream butter until light. Add vanilla and egg yolks, one at a time. Stir in chocolate and hazelnuts. Whip egg whites with salt until soft peaks form. Fold into batter. Turn into pans. Bake 25 minutes. Cool.

■ To make the icing: heat coffee in a small saucepan over low heat. Add chocolate and let it melt, stirring occasionally. Cool. Cream butter with sugar until light. Add egg yolks, one at a time. Stir in cooled chocolate. Brush the cooled cake layers with a little Frangelico. Spread one layer with some of the icing. Top with second layer, spread with remaining icing. Or, you could put a little of it in a piping bag with a star tip, and use it to decorate the base and the top edge of the cake with little rosettes.

Ilona Torte is one of the most often requested desserts at Chez Grandmère, a chocolate cake flavored with roasted hazelnuts. Hazelnuts and chocolate are really made to go together, a fact evidently appreciated by a great number of our patrons.

Shrimp in Curry-Mango Sauce

SERVES 10

SAUCE

3 T Oil
1 Onion, medium
1 Apple, cored
1 Banana, large and ripe
1 Tomato
2 Cloves garlic
Salt and pepper
3 T Curry
1 t Turmeric
Pinch thyme
Pinch nutmeg
2 Bay leaves
3 T Flour
1 qt Chicken stock
1 Large, or 2 medium mangos, peeled and puréed (or 3 good tablespoons of mango chutney)
2 oz Coconut milk or cream

Make the sauce: heat the oil in a medium saucepan and add diced onion, apple, banana, tomato and garlic. Sauté until almost puréed. Meanwhile, mix all dry spices together. Then add spice mixture to fruit mixture in saucepan. Mix very well. Cook, stirring often over medium heat for 5 minutes. Then add flour and again cook over medium heat for 5 minutes. It will form a rough paste. Then add warm stock and mix very well. Let simmer for 30 minutes. Salt and pepper to taste. Add puréed mangos or chutney. Let simmer for 10 more minutes. Strain through fine strainer. Add coconut milk or cream. If not thick enough, add a little cornstarch mixed in water until desired thickness.

■ Make the shrimp: preheat oven to 400 degrees. Peel and devein shrimp. Take tomatoes and from end to end on their underside, make slit. Bring water to a boil, and submerse tomatoes for 30 seconds-do not over cook. Dip in cool water, and remove skins. With sharp knife, slice tomatoes into ½" wide slices. Use only the outer meaty parts of the tomatoes, not the seedy insides. Cut the strips into 3" pieces. Wrap each shrimp with a strip of tomato.

SHRIMP

40-48 Medium-large shrimp
10 Tomatoes
Boiling water
½ C White wine
2 oz Butter

GARNISH

1 Mango
1 Fresh lime

Recipe continued on the following page

■ In a baking sheet or pan, line the bottom with foil. When cutting foil, cut a piece twice as long as the sheet or pan. Note: ½ of the foil will line the pan, and at this point, the other ½ will be hanging over the pan. Place shrimp on pan, pour white wine and sprinkle with butter. Take the excess foil and fold it back over the pan and shrimp. Seal edges of foil. Put in oven for about 10-12 minutes until thoroughly steamed, but still firm to the touch.

■ To serve: on warmed plates, pour curry-mango sauce. Arrange shrimp and mango slices (that have been sprinkled with fresh lime) on top of sauce.

Wine Suggestion: Puligny Montrachet, Leflavie Clavillon, 1983. A French White Burgundy.

Sweetbreads with Figs and Fresh Mint

SERVES 8

2 ½ lbs Calves'
    sweetbreads
1 Large onion, peeled,
    cut in half
6 Whole cloves
1 Large bunch fresh
    mint
¾ C Unsalted butter
2 Large carrots, pared,
    cut into 1" pieces
2 Bay leaves
1 ¼ C Dry vermouth
2 ½ C (or as needed)
    Water
1 C Dry white wine
1 C Sugar
8 Fresh figs, preferably
    purple *
3 T All-purpose flour
3 T Unsalted butter
¼ C Heavy cream
1-2 T Fresh lemon juice
Freshly ground pepper

One day before serving, soak sweetbreads in 3 changes of cold water in refrigerator at least 4 hours. Drain thoroughly. Stud onion halves with cloves. Measure 1 cup (packed) mint leaves and reserve. Reserve 8 perfect small mint leaves for garnish. Heat ¾ cup butter in medium Dutch oven over medium-high heat. When foam subsides, add carrots; sauté, stirring constantly, 2 minutes. Reduce heat to medium-low; cook uncovered until carrots are soft, about 10 minutes. Remove pan from heat and add sweetbreads, onion halves, bay leaves and 1 cup mint leaves. Pour vermouth and 2 cups water over sweetbreads. Add more water if needed to cover sweetbreads by ¼". Heat over high heat to boiling. Reduce heat to medium-low; gently simmer uncovered, turning sweetbreads once half-way through cooking time, 1 hour. Transfer sweetbreads to large bowl of ice water and let cool about 10 minutes.

■ Meanwhile, strain and measure 3 cups cooking liquid. Let cool to room temperature. Remove outer membrane, any fat, and connecting tubes from sweetbreads. Cut away dark spots if necessary. Gently pull lobes apart into 1" pieces. Cover sweetbreads with dampened paper towels as you work to prevent them from drying. Return sweetbreads to cooled stock and refrigerate covered overnight. The following day, heat remaining ½ cup water, the white wine, and sugar to boiling in medium saucepan over medium-high heat. Add figs and reduce heat to medium-low. Simmer until figs are slightly softened, about 3 minutes. Drain figs and cover with foil to keep warm. *Recipe continued.*

■ Cook flour and 3 tablespoons butter, stirring constantly, in heavy medium saucepan over medium heat 5 minutes. Do not allow to brown. Heat oven to 200 degrees. Remove sweetbreads in cooking liquid from refrigerator and spoon off congealed fat. Heat to boiling over medium-high heat. Reduce heat to low; simmer 3 minutes. Strain liquid into medium saucepan. Cover sweetbreads with dampened paper towel and keep warm in oven.

■ Heat flour-butter mixture over medium-high heat. Gradually whisk in hot strained liquid. Heat to boiling. Reduce heat to medium-low, simmer, skimming surface frequently, until sauce coats back of metal spoon, 10-15 minutes. Whisk in cream; heat to boiling. Stir in 1 tablespoon lemon juice. Season to taste with salt and freshly ground pepper and additional lemon juice if desired. Spoon sweetbreads into 8 warmed individual ramekins. Ladle about ¼ cup sauce over sweetbreads. Place 1 fig in each ramekin and top each serving with reserved mint leaf. Serve immediately.

Wine Suggestion: 1985, Sonoma Cutrer, Chardonnay; Les Pierres Vineyards, Russian River Valley.

*Dried figs can be substituted for the fresh if necessary. Reduce sugar in poaching liquid for figs to ¾ cup and poach dried figs until soft, about 10 minutes longer.

Shavano's

THIS SNOWMASS RESTAURANT IS NAMED AFTER SHAVANO, an Uncompahagre Ute Indian chief, and Mt. Shavano, the tenth highest mountain in Colorado, located on the continental divide near Salida. The name suggests a comfortable, Colorado restaurant.

Chef and co-owner Teddy Lawrence serves creative American and classical cuisine. The menu changes nightly in the winter in order to remain appealing, because many tourists enjoy dining at Shavano's often during their vacation. The summer menu changes periodically and features nightly specials. They offer a wide variety of fresh fish with innovative sauces, lamb, veal, steak, duck and chicken. An extensive California wine list complements their menu.

Owners Sue Lyn and Teddy Lawrence created Shavano's in 1983 after previous involvement with The Peppermill and Krabloonik.

The decor consists of pine woodwork with a burgundy color scheme. Their unusual bar, with a stained glass backdrop and a marble surface, is a prominent feature.

Shavano's can be romantic. It can be relaxing or it can be fun with a group. But more importantly, it is Shavano's varied creative cuisine that keeps their patrons returning time and time again.

Bittersweet Chocolate Expresso Cheesecake

CRUST
1 ½ C Graham cracker crumbs
1 Stick butter, melted

FILLING
1 ½ lb Cream cheese
½ C Sugar
½ C Whipping cream
6 oz Unsweetened chocolate
½ C Expresso coffee (instant expresso works)
4 Whole eggs
½ C Sugar

TOPPING
12 oz Sour cream
3 T-3 oz Creme de Cocoa or Grand Marnier (to taste)
¼ C Sugar

To make the crust: combine and mix the graham cracker crumbs and butter and press into bottom of 10" springform pan.

■ To make the filling: blend first 3 ingredients in mixer until smooth. Melt the chocolate and expresso over low heat. Beat eggs and sugar with hand beater, Cuisinart or mixer until fluffy.

■ Add the chocolate mixture to the cream cheese mixture, then add the egg mixture. Blend well, scraping sides of bowl. Pour mixture into springform pan and bake in 300 degrees oven for approximately 1 hour and 15 minutes (or until toothpick comes out clean). Turn oven off, prop door open and let sit for ½ hour. Cool at room temperature.

■ To make the topping: mix topping ingredients well in bowl by hand. Pour over cheesecake (will be sunken slightly in middle) and bake at 400 degrees for 10-15 minutes. Let cool at room temperature for ½ hour, then refrigerate. Garnish Creme de Cocoa topping with shredded sweet chocolate. Garnish Grand Marnier with shredded orange zest.

Fried Brie with Fresh Berries

½ of 1 kg. wheel of brie
(preferably 50%), cut
in 6 pieces; herbed
brie, peppered brie or
a firm Camembert
may be used.
3 Eggs, beaten well
1 C Flour
2 C Bread crumbs
(approximately)
Oil (Crisco works well)
Fresh berries (your
choice)

Set up an assembly line: flour, egg wash, then
crumbs. Roll brie in flour, shake off excess, coat
well with egg wash, then immediately coat and
pack with bread crumbs. If any bare spots are
showing, dip in egg wash and bread crumbs
again. Chill.

■ Fry in 400 degrees oil for about 10-15 seconds. A small saucepan with a couple of inches
of oil over a medium to medium-high heat
works well. If oil is smoking, it is too hot.

■ Serve with fresh raspberries, blackberries,
boysenberries or any combination of fruit and
toast points. Makes a great appetizer or dessert.

The kicker: for a beautiful presentation, serve on
a silver platter and garnish with fresh flowers!

The Stew Pot

FROM THE MOMENT YOU WALK IN THE DOOR OF THE Stew Pot restaurant, you immediately feel at home, Its casual, relaxed atmosphere is complemented with the savory aromas coming from the kitchen. It's no wonder that when visitors arrive in Snowmass, the first thing they want to do is go to this tiny eatery on the mall for a home-cooked meal.

Originally owned by Bob and Ruth Kevan, the basic concept remains—to appeal to skiers' hearty appetites. James "Rob" Robinson has owned and operated The Stew Pot for 13 years and has fed hungry skiers, hikers, rafters and balloonists in a style befitting to their athletic endeavors.

They serve two homemade soups and two-three stews each day. Rob explains, "Our most popular soups are New England Clam Chowder and Tomato Soup topped with grated cheese. Our Belgium beef stew, in beer gravy sauce with mushrooms and potatoes, is also a favorite." Rob is very proud of his head chef, Barry Barth and his innovative cooking skills. It's a close-knit operation with Barry's brother, Chuck, and Rob's sister-in-law, Betsy, as floor managers.

Their honey wheat bread is a constant source of enjoyment to their patrons. They bake bread twice daily and the divine sniffs elicit praise from passersby and delight customers already seated.

The winter menu now includes a variety of fresh salads and sandwiches, and the summer menu offers a lovely fresh fruit plate that's refreshing on a hot day.

To satisfy the constant flow of people demanding their ice cream, Rob consented and built a take-out window. After a long winter, locals and visitors enjoy dining on their large outdoor patio, surrounded by flowers.

Beef Curry Stew

SERVES 8-10

3 ½ lbs Stew meat
1 Medium onion,
  chopped
3 T Oil
1 T Butter
½ C White flour
½ C White wine
3 Celery stalks, cut into
  ½" strips
2 Large carrots, cut
  into ¼" slices
1 T Curry powder
½ t Ginger
Dash Worcestershire
3 Beef bouillon cubes
Pinch black pepper
1 t Grey Poupon
  mustard
5 Potatoes, cut into
  small chunks
1 C Sour cream
Parsley flakes

In a medium pot, add first 4 ingredients and brown together. Stir in flour and mix with meat to form a roux. Add wine, celery and carrots. Cover these ingredients with water. Season with next 6 ingredients. Cover pot and cook for 3 hours on medium heat. Add potatoes and cook ½ hour more. Add sour cream. Serve hot with a garnish of parsley flakes.

Wine Suggestion: Sebastiani Chardonnay.

Stew Pot's Homemade Honey Wheat Bread

MAKES 2 LOAVES

2 T Vegetable oil
1/4 C Honey
1 T Molasses
Dash cinnamon
3 t Salt
1 C Hot water
1 C Cold water
2 T Dry yeast
3 C Wheat flour
2 1/4 C White flour

Mix together first 6 ingredients and stir until all is dissolved. Add 1 cup cold water which will bring the mixture to a lukewarm temperature. Add the yeast and stir vigorously to activate it. Add all wheat flour and 1 cup white flour. Knead together until all the flour is incorporated with the liquid. Then add remaining 1 1/4 cup white flour and knead until there is no flour visible. Let proof for one hour. Punch down. Place in 2 oiled 9" X 3" bread pans and let proof 10-15 minutes. Bake at 325 degrees for 1 hour.

The Windstar Foundation

LTHOUGH NOT A RESTAURANT, THE WINDSTAR
Foundation is an integral part of the Aspen/Snowmass Valley.
During their educational workshops, Windstar serves
vegetarian, organically grown, unbelievably delicious feasts to its
participants. I felt Windstar should be included in this cookbook as a
tribute to an energetic foundation trying to better this planet we live on.

Imagine three wonderful, unconventional, vegetarian meals served
among good friends. This is what awaits you if you enroll in any number
of Windstar workshops.

The large, homey kitchen is the center of activity. Few can avoid
dropping in "for just a minute" to savor the smells coming from the
oven. The traditional Windstar bread is baking and mouths are watering,
waiting to cherish a bite.

Emma Walling, the head chef, came to Windstar as a volunteer and
never left. She's "like everyone's mother." Emma is making spanikopita
(a Greek favorite) for lunch. She's also putting the finishing touches on a
huge salad. All the ingredients were picked five minutes earlier from the
lush garden outside. Talk about fresh! She'll toss the salad with homemade miso dressing. The carrot cake (yes, made with carrots from their
garden) and date cookies are cooling for dessert. The combination of
aromas drive both the workshop participants and the staffers wild.

Emma rings the dinner bell, people drop everything and come running; waiting to have their appetites satisfied.

First, as is the tradition at Windstar, everyone joins hands in a circle
for a moment of thanksgiving before the meal. Then, it's time to sit
down and eat and chat about the day's progress. A sense of camaraderie
has formed and the meal is relaxed and enjoyable with bouts of uncon-
trollable laughter.

There are always the comments from meat and potato eaters: "How
can this food taste so good with no meat?" Emma knows how to dazzle
anyone with her ability to combine the freshest ingredients in a creative
style. The results are appreciated by all.

Looking outside to the sun glistening on the 50 foot Biodome, one wonders just what it is they do here at Windstar. Founded by John Denver and Thomas Crum, Windstar is a non-profit education and demonstration center. Workshops provide on-site programs in renewable energy and food production technologies, land stewardship and global resource management, conflict resolution, international citizen exchange and personal and community growth.

Carrot Cake

MAKES 1 CAKE USING A 9" X 13" PAN

CAKE
2 ½ C Grated carrots, firmly packed
3 T Lemon juice
1 t Grated lemon peel
2 C Whole wheat pastry flour
2 t Baking powder
1 t Sea salt
2 t Cinnamon
¼ t Allspice
⅛ t Nutmeg
⅛ t Cloves
¾ C Safflower oil
¾ C Honey
2 t Vanilla extract
4 Eggs, well beaten
¾ C Coconut
¾ C Raisins

FROSTING
⅔ C Cream cheese, softened
3 T Butter, softened
2 ½ T Pure maple syrup
½ t Vanilla extract
¾ C Chopped walnuts

Preheat oven to 350 degrees. In a bowl, combine carrots, lemon juice and peel. Set aside. In another bowl, combine flour, baking powder, salt and spices. Set aside. In a large mixing bowl, combine oil, honey and vanilla. Add the beaten eggs. Add dry ingredients to wet ingredients and mix thoroughly. Fold in carrots, coconut and raisins. Turn into a well-oiled pan. Bake for 1 hour or until cake tests done. Cool completely before frosting.

■ To make frosting: cream together cream cheese and butter. Add maple syrup and vanilla. Blend well. Spread frosting onto cake and sprinkle with walnuts.

Quinoa Muffins

MAKES 1 DOZEN

1 C Whole wheat flour
½ C Rice flour
¼ C Powdered milk
2 t Baking powder
¾ t Sea salt
¼ C Safflower oil
3 T Barley malt
1 C Warm water
1 Egg, beaten
1 C Cooked quinoa or
   brown rice

Preheat oven to 400 degrees. In a large mixing bowl, combine first 5 ingredients and set aside. In another bowl, combine next 5 ingredients and mix well. Using a wire whisk, quickly stir wet ingredients into dry ingredients. Do not over-mix. Spoon into a well-oiled muffin pan and bake for about 20 minutes. Let cool 5 minutes before removing from pan.

Quinoa (pronounced "keenwa") is the highest in protein content of all the world's grains.

Spinach Lasagna

SERVES 8

1 Recipe Italian sauce
  (recipe follows)
1 ½ lbs Fresh spinach
1 lb Firm tofu, drained
  well on paper towels
1 lb Creamed, low fat
  cottage cheese
¼ C Grated Parmesan
  cheese
½ C Fresh chopped
  parsley
1 t Vege-sal or to taste
Pepper to taste
1 C Grated Monterey
  Jack cheese
¾ lb Sesame or spinach
  lasagna noodles
1 T Olive oil
¾ lb Grated Mozzarella
  cheese
Oregano

ITALIAN SAUCE
¼ C Olive oil
4 Large cloves garlic,
  minced
1 Small onion, chopped

2 Small bay leaves
4 t Dried basil
1 ½ t Oregano
1 6 oz Can tomato
  paste
1 28 oz Can crushed
  tomatoes
1 14 oz Can diced
  tomatoes
2 T Fresh chopped
  parsley
½ t Sea salt or to taste
¼ t Pepper or to taste
½ t Honey
Dash tamari
½ lb Mushrooms, sliced

First make the sauce: sauté garlic and onions in heated oil for a few minutes until tender. Add bay leaves, basil and oregano. Lower heat and stir in tomato paste, blending well. Add next 7 ingredients. Simmer over low heat for about 30 minutes, stirring occasionally. Add sliced mushrooms and simmer for another 20 minutes. If sauce is too thick for your taste, thin with water. Adjust seasonings to taste.

■ Wash, stem and steam spinach. Do not overcook. Drain well. In a bowl, crumble tofu. Add cottage cheese and blend together. Add the next 5 ingredients and mix well. Cook lasagna noodles al dente in lightly salted water to which 1 tablespoon of oil has been added. Keep covered in cold water until ready to use.

Recipe continued
on the following page

. . . .

■ In a lasagna pan or large casserole dish, spread 1 cup of sauce. Arrange a flat layer of noodles on sauce, and spread another ¾ cup of sauce on noodles. Sprinkle cheese mixture on top and add a little Mozzarella cheese. Arrange spinach and cover with 1 cup sauce. Layer remaining noodles, smother with sauce and top with Mozzarella cheese. Sprinkle with oregano. Cover loosely with foil and bake in a pre-heated 350 degrees oven for 50 minutes. Uncover and bake another 10 minutes or until hot and bubbly. Remove from oven and let sit for about 5 minutes before serving.

The kicker: you can substitute 2 pounds of ricotta cheese for tofu and cottage cheese. You might want to double this recipe because it freezes so well.

Windstar Bread

MAKES 2 LARGE, ROUND, BRAIDED LOAVES

2 T Baking yeast
¾ C Warm water
1 13 ounce can
   evaporated milk
¾ t Sea salt
½ C Honey
1 ½ C Boiling water
1 C Unbleached white
   flour
7-8 C Whole wheat
   flour
Butter

In a small glass bowl, activate yeast in warm water for 5-10 minutes. In a large mixing bowl, whisk together milk, salt, honey and boiling water. Add activated yeast and mix well. Whisk in (1 cup at a time) 4 cups whole wheat flour, 1 cup white flour and 2 more cups of whole wheat flour. Knead in 1 ½ cups flour until dough no longer is sticky or adheres to your hands. On a well-floured surface, knead in more flour until dough is smooth and elastic. Let rest 10 minutes.

■ Generously butter two 10" pie pans. Cut dough in half. Working one half at a time, knead for about 5 more minutes and cut into 3 sections. On a lightly-floured surface, roll each section into a snake approximately 18" long. Connect the 3 snakes at the top and braid. Shape braid into a ring. Place braided ring into a buttered pie pan. Cover with a towel and let rise in a warm place for 30 minutes. Repeat the above process for the other half. Bake in a pre-heated 350 degrees oven for 35 minutes or until golden brown. Remove from pans immediately. Brush with butter if desired.

Bonnie's

THE DECK OF BONNIE'S ON A SUNNY WARM DAY, FILLED with skiers clad in a spectrum of colors, reminds you of many ocean-side, California restaurants. It has that relaxed, "let's have a bottle of wine and enjoy ourselves" feeling. Everyone is smiling and joking.

Located two-thirds of the way up Aspen Mountain, Bonnie's is at the base of Tourtlelotte Park. Bonnie, along with partners Mary Anne and Peter Greene, has owned the restaurant since 1980. It was previously Gretl's. Their goal, when they took over ownership, was to make it even better. Bonnie explains, "Gretl is a dear friend and she was a tough act to follow!" They have continued her tradition of serving only fresh foods, using the best ingredients and starting from scratch.

Locals and tourists flock to Bonnie's for her homemade desserts, including strudl (her own variation), apple dumplings, cakes and pies—all topped with freshly whipped cream, if you desire. One of their most popular items is their pizza. They pride themselves on never making the same pizza twice. Choose from either a meat or a vegetarian pizza with generous and imaginative toppings.

Bonnie allows her chefs and bakers the freedom to show their creativity in order for them to stay fresh and enthusiastic throughout the ski season. They serve a chicken chowder and chili daily along with a soup of the day. Their homemade French bread as an accompaniment is a must. Although the Caesar and spinach salads are most popular, they also offer other varieties to satisfy their steady clientele.

To complement Bonnie's food is an extensive wine list. Skiers are a hearty bunch who are known to have a good time. What better way to spend a lunch hour than to eat a fine meal with a great bottle of wine and people-watch! After all, Bonnie's is *the* place to be on Aspen Mountain.

Bonnie's Caesar Salad Dressing

In a Mixmaster, not a blender or Cuisinart, mix first 4 ingredients. Dissolve it with the egg yolks and very slowly add the 4 oils. Turn mixer off and add the last 7 ingredients all together. Use Romaine lettuce with homemade garlic croutons. Note: see the Chart House's recipe for croutons.

MAKES 1 QUART

2 T Sugar
2 T Salt
3 T Dry Mustard
4 T Good quality red wine vinegar
2 Egg yolks
1 Pint Wesson oil
1 C Garlic oil (keep on hand in your refrigerator-vegetable oil with lots of garlic cloves) or 1 C Wesson oil mixed with 4 pressed garlic cloves

2 C Olive oil
½ C Wesson oil
¾ C Wine vinegar
1 T Tabasco
1 T Worcestershire
2 T Coarsely ground black pepper
6 T Lemon juice
1 Can chopped anchovies
1 C Parmesan, freshly grated

Bonnie's Haywood County Plum Cake

1 C plus 3 T Sugar
1 C Vegetable oil
3 Eggs
1 t Vanilla
2 C Flour
1 t each-Baking soda,
   nutmeg, allspice,
   cinnamon
1/4 t Salt
1 1/4 C Buttermilk
1 C Pecans, chopped
1 C Cooked prunes,
   chopped (you can use
   canned plums or I
   like cooked Italian
   prunes found in the
   grocery in August)

TOPPING
1 C Sugar
1/2 C Buttermilk
1/4 C Butter
1 T Corn syrup
1 t each-Baking soda
   and vanilla

Blend sugar and oil, then add eggs one at a time mixing well after each addition. Add vanilla. Add sifted dry ingredients alternately with buttermilk. Stir in nuts and plums. Pour batter in 9" X 9" X 2" pan. Bake in 325 degrees oven 40-50 minutes.

■ Combine topping ingredients in saucepan and cook over low heat until sugar is dissolved. Cook the icing for a few minutes more until it thickens. With a skewer, prick the hot cake and pour the icing over the cake adding more icing as it is absorbed. Cut the cake in the pan.

Bonnie's West Indies Chicken Salad

Mix first 5 ingredients. Add bananas and peanuts just before serving.

Wine Suggestion: Cakebread, Sauvignon Blanc.

SERVES 4

1 ¼ lb Cooked chicken breast, diced in 1" cubes

1 Medium red delicious apple, cut in 1" cubes

3 Celery stalks, chopped

⅔ C Major Grey's chutney

¾ C Mayonnaise

2 Bananas, sliced

1 C Virginia peanuts

Café Suzanne

CAFÉ SUZANNE IS A CHARMING LITTLE RESTAURANT, located at the base of the West Buttermilk lift. Serving only lunch, they cater to both downhill and cross-country skiers—as the Government Trail begins just above the restaurant. Non-skiers may also eat at Café Suzanne by simply driving up the West Buttermilk road.

Owners Susan and Doug McPherson have created a French country atmosphere to complement their primarily French menu. Susan is a collector and has decorated the restaurant with things she's picked up all over Europe. "Since I spend so much of my time here, I like to be surrounded by things I'm fond of. I mostly shop at street markets and thrift shops, where I often find incredible treasures."

Unique to any mountain restaurant in this area, Café Suzanne does not serve hamburgers or hot dogs. Instead, they offer French-style crêpes, which customers enjoy as a change from the ordinary. Choose from three luncheon crêpes (spinach, ham and cheese or chicken) and three dessert crêpes (Grand Marnier, raspberry or apples and cinnamon). The batter is made from buckwheat flour, which is the traditional crêpe from Normandy, France. They're made fresh daily.

Their menu offers homemade soups, salads, Croque Monsieurs (a French sandwich of grilled ham and Gruyère cheese with dijon mustard) and specials. Susan explains, "Because we're such a small operation, we have the option of changing our specials daily. I trust my employees' creativity. Stuffed Cornish game hens and Pierre Lapin are examples of their choices."

Beside the dessert crêpes, Susan satisfies her customers with ravishing sweets. Her cheesecake, brownies, carrot cake, fudge cake, tarts and pies are incredibly delicious.

Since their restaurant seats only 70 people, Susan and Doug have incorporated the method of seating used in French bistros and cafés—Au Banquette. Their picnic tables are both intimate and practical.

The McPhersons' talents complement each other. Susan works culinary magic and Doug handles the wines. Wine is his love and he chooses mostly French wines at affordable prices. Wine with crêpes is a lovely traditional combination.

Cheesecake

2 C Cookie or cracker
   crumbs (of your
   choice)
1⅓ C Sugar
6 T Butter, melted
1 ½ lbs Softened cream
   cheese
4 Eggs
⅓ C Heavy cream
¼ C Liqueur (of your
   choice)
1 t Vanilla
2 C Sour cream
1 T Sugar
1 t Vanilla

In a food processor, finely grind the cookie or cracker crumbs. Add ⅓ cup sugar, then slowly add up to 6 tablespoons butter (while processor is running) until the crumbs are moistened and hold together. Pat the mixture into a buttered 9 ½" springform pan (take care not to have the inside corner too thick) and go up the sides ½ the distance.

■ In a mixer, cream together the softened cream cheese and 1 cup sugar. When well mixed, add the eggs, one at a time. Again mix well. Add the next 3 ingredients and beat until light. Pour into the shell and bake at 375 degrees for 30 minutes. Remove from the oven and let stand for 5 minutes. Combine the last 3 ingredients and spread on cake, then return to oven for 5 minutes. Chill, lightly covered, overnight.

Lentil Soup

SERVES 8

Red wine
2 lbs Lentils
2 Ham hocks
4 Medium yellow
  onions, chopped
  roughly
6 Stalks celery (use
  tops), chopped
6 Carrots, chopped
3 Cloves garlic, crushed
2 T Parsley, chopped
1 Large can diced
  tomatoes
2 Packages frozen
  chopped spinach
1 ½ t Thyme
2 Bay leaves
Salt and pepper

Throw all ingredients in a large pot with a mixture of ⅓ red wine and ⅔ water to cover these ingredients. Bring to a boil and then simmer for at least 3 hours. Pick meat off of hocks and return meat to pot. Season to taste.

The kicker: this soup grows as it cooks. Add the liquid as it cooks, more wine, water or vegetable stock until it is the consistency that you prefer. This freezes well.

Pierre Lapin

SERVES 4

1 Rabbit (about 4 lbs)
   order from your
   butcher
2 T Butter
¼ lb Lean Bacon, diced
3 T Brandy
¼ C Flour
1 C Beef bouillon
1 C Dry white wine
3 Cloves crushed garlic
1 Bay leaf
1 t of each-chopped
   parsley, leaf oregano
   and thyme
1 Can small onions
   (can use pearl
   onions)
¾ lb Mushrooms, sliced

Joint the rabbit as you would a chicken, except for the back. Bugialli's "Classic Techniques of Italian Cooking" has detailed instructions and pictures of the process.

■ Brown and reserve the bacon in a separate container. Add rabbit to fat in pan and brown. When browned, add the brandy (make sure it's warm first) and ignite. Add flour and stir into rabbit for a minute. Blend bouillon, wine, garlic and herbs and pour over rabbit. Simmer for 1 hour. Add the reserved bacon, mushrooms and onions. Simmer another ½ hour or until fork tender. Note: Using a slow simmer, the rabbit will be done after about 1 hour. Salt and pepper to taste.

Wine Suggestion: 1981 Sonoma Cutrer, Chardonnay; Les Pierres Vineyard.

Gretl's

THIS COOKBOOK COULD NOT BE COMPLETE WITHOUT including Gretl, her world-famous restaurant and four of her favorite recipes.

I'm sitting in Gretl's homey kitchen sipping tea and reminiscing of days past, as the intense aroma of apple strudl permeates the air. How can anyone forget Gretl's apple strudl, made from scratch and served piping hot with a clump of whipped cream. It's legendary! It was served at her restaurant, Gretl's, perched halfway up Aspen Mountain.

It all began in December of 1966, when Gretl's dream of owning her own restaurant came true. Gretl had observed over the years, the need for a European-style restaurant that would cater to those who loved to eat great food. Her family had owned and operated such a restaurant in Garmisch-Partenkirchen, Germany.

Gretl was appalled at the restaurants that were serving canned soups and packaged foods. "I wanted to serve my customers only the best—everything fresh." Gretl's became unique; people responded to her home cooking and Gretl's popularity made it *the* place to go for the best food anywhere. Gretl developed her own recipe for apple strudl and it was an instant hit. People loved it, they stood in long lines for it, they dreamt about it, they reserved it and they ordered it from such faraway places as Washington, D.C. This delicious concoction of homemade pastry, wrapped around apples (cored and peeled by hand), had customers dazzled. The recipe remains a secret.

Gretl's other desserts that had customers drooling were: cream puffs, trifle, apple cake and streussl.

Her other specialties should not be overlooked. Her soups changed daily and on any given day you might find: butter or liver dumpling, cauliflower, tomato, broccoli or zucchini. "I do not believe in mystery soups," Gretl explains, "you should be able to taste the main vegetable." Gretl tells us her secret to the success of her soups. "Just before serving the soup, blend two egg yolks with ½ pint of heavy cream (for eight servings of soup) and add to the soup mixture. Do not boil. This will make the soup thick and delicious."

Each dish looked better than the next because Gretl believes, "You eat with your eyes."

Gretl's last year on Aspen Mountain was the spring of 1980. Now, she does consultation for the Merry-Go-Round and Cloud 9 restaurants on Aspen Highlands. You'll be happy to know you can still get Gretl's strudl and many of her other delights at the Highlands.

Gretl has wonderful memories of her restaurant on Aspen Mountain, and we have many fond memories of her.

Apple Streussl

PASTRY
1 ½ C Unbleached flour
⅓ C Sugar
4 Egg yolks
½ C plus 2 T Unsalted
   butter
½ t Almond extract

FILLING
2 lbs Tart, crisp apples
1 T Lemon juice
1 T Brown sugar
1 t Cinnamon

TOPPING
1 ½ Sticks unsalted
   butter
1 C Flour
1 C Brown sugar
1 t Cinnamon
Powdered sugar

Preheat oven to 400 degrees. Mix all pastry ingredients and knead on a board. Roll out ⅔ of dough. Take ring off 10", greased springform pan and place dough on bottom of pan and bake 15 minutes. Form finger-thick rolls from rest of dough to place around the inside of the ring before filling.

■ Peel, core and slice apples. Toss apples with sugar and lemon juice. Add cinnamon. Fill prebaked shell. Make the topping: cut the butter into small slices. Place flour, sugar and cinnamon in a large bowl. Work quickly so butter does not melt. Use pastry cutter until mixed together, continue until all flour and sugar is incorporated into butter and streussl is loose and crumbly. Crumble over apple filling. Bake at 375 degrees for 50 minutes to 1 hour. Let cool. Dust with powdered sugar.

Haselnuss Torte

BATTER

8 Egg yolks
1 ¼ C Sugar
Grated peel of lemon
⅓ C Cake flour
3 C Finely ground
filberts (almonds)
8 Egg whites
1 C Apricot preserves

FROSTING

4 oz Semi-sweet
chocolate
½ oz Unsweetened
chocolate
1 Stick unsalted butter
1 t Vanilla, or 1 T rum
or cognac, or ¼ t
almond extract

Preheat oven to 350 degrees. Butter and flour a 9" springform pan. Line the bottom with wax paper and spray lightly with Baker's Joy. Beat egg yolks with sugar until creamy. Add lemon peel. In a separate bowl, beat egg whites until stiff, fold the flour into egg-sugar mixture, follow with egg whites and filberts, very gently.

■ Immediately pour batter into prepared pan and bake in oven for 50-60 minutes or until a cake tester inserted comes out clean. Let cake rest for 5 minutes before unmolding it onto a cake rack. Cool completely before applying frosting. With a pastry brush, coat torte with hot preserves. Allow to dry.

■ In double boiler, over barely simmering water, melt the chocolate. Turn off heat and whisk in butter. When smooth, add some flavoring (vanilla, rum, cognac or almond). Let cool to spreading consistency. Spread frosting evenly over top and sides. Needs several hours to set. Decorate.

The kicker: Gretl warns you if you make this on a day when the barometer is dropping, bake for an extra 10 minutes!

Red Currant Tart

4 ½ C Red Currants, remove stems
4 Egg whites
1 ¼ C Sugar
1 t Vanilla
1 C Almonds, finely ground, unblanched

Preheat oven to 400 degrees. Make a partially baked pastry shell, using a 10" springform pan (see Apple Streussl page 165). Wash and drain red currants in a colander and set aside. To make the meringue: beat egg whites until foamy. Add sugar gradually. Continue beating until stiff peaks form. By hand, gently fold in almonds. Fold in currants. Pour meringue mixture into partially baked shell. Bake immediately on low rack for 45 minutes. The tart is done when the meringue is set and browned. Cool in pan. Unbuckle the rim of pan, let stand awhile. Unmold onto cake rack to cool thoroughly.

Trifle

BATTER

8 *Egg yolks*
6-8 T *Lukewarm water*
1 ½ C *Sugar*
2 t *Vanilla*
8 *Egg whites*
2 C *Cake flour, sifted*

FILLING

2 *Packages regular*
   vanilla pudding
Raspberry preserves
½ C *Dry sherry*
Sliced almonds
1 *Pint Whipping cream*
¼ C *Sugar*

Preheat oven to 375 degrees. Line two 14" X 9" X 1" pans with baking parchment or wax paper and butter the bottoms lightly. Beat egg yolks with vanilla, water and half the sugar until thick and lemon-colored. Beat egg whites with rest of sugar until stiff. Add cake flour on top of beaten yolk mixture. Then, fold in beaten egg whites into the yolk-flour mixture.

■ Pour the batter into prepared baking pans and bake for 20-30 minutes (check very carefully). Unmold cake immediately onto wax paper, sprinkled with sugar. Let cool.

■ Follow the directions for making vanilla pudding. Let cool. Put one cake back into baking pan or clear Plexiglas pan. Take ½ cup sherry and drip over cake. Spread raspberry preserves next. Pour half of pudding and spread. Sprinkle sliced almonds over all. Lay second cake on top and repeat with rest of filling. Whip cream with sugar, spread half of it over cake, use other half to decorate and sprinkle once more with some almonds. Let stand overnight before serving.

Gwyn's

LOCATED WITHIN THE HIGH ALPINE RESTAURANT IS A charming, European-style sit-down restaurant complete with linen tablecloths, china place settings and flowers.

Skiers who come to Gwyn's treat themselves to an unforgettable experience. The service is friendly and professional. Their creative menu offers a wide variety of items, complemented by an extensive wine list.

It's quite amazing when you take into consideration the fact that all the supplies must come up to the restaurant's 10,000 foot elevation by snowcat.

Everything is homemade from the soups to the desserts. Only the freshest of ingredients are used to assure the highest quality.

Maybe that's why customers, during the height of the season, are willing to wait hours to eat at Gwyn's!

They're open for breakfast and lunch. Breakfast begins at 9 am and is a great way to start the day and beat the crowds. Sit down to a hot cup of Kona coffee and a basket of freshly baked muffins. The most popular items on the breakfast menu are: fresh fruit pancakes, Alpine Potatoes, Zucchini Fritatta, Eggs Benedict and Huevos.

Lunch offers, in addition to their regular menu, a daily special list that allows the chefs to be creative. The fresh fish varies daily and the sauces change with the chefs' whims. Following are examples of the special list: grilled Hawaiian Ahi with papaya butter, poached Norwegian Salmon with fresh raspberry cream sauce. Pacific Stonecrab and Wild Mushroom fettuccine and New Zealand Emerald Mussels.

Not many can pass up Gwyn's dessert tray, beautifully garnished with flowers. A selection may include: Poppyseed Torte, Chocolate Mousse Tart, White Chocolate and Chocolate Chip Ice Cream with linzer stars, Fresh Fruit Tart with kiwis, star fruit and raspberries and Chocolate Gâteau.

Ski Magazine boasts of Gwyn's "...one of the handful of U.S. mountain restaurants on a par with the better European ones."

Chocolate Gâteau

SERVES 6

1 ½ t Instant espresso
2 T Hot water
2 T Rum
7 oz Semi-sweet
    chocolate
1 oz Unsweetened
    chocolate
3 Large eggs
¼ C Sugar
½ C Whip cream
1 ½ t Vanilla
Whip cream
Chocolate shavings

Preheat oven to 350 degrees. Melt the first 5 ingredients together in a double boiler over low heat. Remove from heat. Beat the eggs and sugar until triple in volume. Set aside. Whip the whip cream and vanilla together until it forms soft peaks. Beat chocolate mixture. Fold in the egg mixture and fold in the whip cream. Spoon the batter into 6 individual ramekins. Set ramekins into a pan filled with water an inch deep. Bake 30 minutes. Serve warm and garnish with a dollop of whip cream and chocolate shavings.

Chocolate Mousse Tart

CRUST
2 ½ C Chocolate wafers, crushed
4-8 T Butter, melted

FILLING
4 Egg yolks
¾ C Sugar
¼ C Kamora, or Kahlua
1 t Vanilla
⅛ t Salt
4 oz Unsweetened chocolate
2 oz Semi-sweet chocolate
6 T Butter
¼ C Espresso
4 Egg whites
2 T Powdered sugar
¾ C Whip cream

TOPPING
6 oz White chocolate
3 ½ T Vegetable oil
1 oz Semi-sweet chocolate

Blend the chocolate wafers and butter together until moistened and press into a 10" pie tin. Chill for 10 minutes. In a double boiler over medium heat, beat the first 5 filling ingredients for 10 minutes until thick and creamy. Set aside in a large mixing bowl. In a double boiler over low heat, melt the chocolate and butter, then stir in warm espresso. Cool and add to the yolk mixture.

■ Beat egg whites and powdered sugar until they form light peaks. Fold into chocolate mixture. Whip the whip cream into soft peaks and fold into above mixture. Pour into crust and chill for 15 minutes. For the topping: melt white chocolate and 3 tablespoons of oil over a bowl of hot water. Keep warm. Over a bowl of very hot water, melt the semi-sweet chocolate and ½ tablespoon of oil. Pour the white chocolate over the chilled tart and immediately pipe a thin spiral of semi-sweet chocolate from the center of the tart. Pull a knife in radials out from the center to make a design. Chill for 2 hours and serve.

Fresh Fruit Tart

CRUST

1 ¼ C Flour
½ t Sugar
½ C Butter, cut into pieces
½ t Salt
¼ t Lemon extract
¼ C Ice water

TART

½ C Sugar
1 C Heavy cream
1 Large egg yolk
1 t Gelatin
1 C Sour cream
1 t Vanilla
1 T Apricot jelly
1 T White wine
2 C Assorted fruit

Preheat oven to 375 degrees. Cut the flour, salt, sugar and butter together until they resemble coarse sand. Add the wet ingredients slowly with food processor running. Form into a ball and refrigerate for 30 minutes. In a double boiler, combine the sugar, cream, yolk and gelatin. Cook for at least 10 minutes until sugar has dissolved. Cool. Beat in the sour cream and vanilla. Roll out the dough and fit into a 10" tart pan. Trim edges. Let rest for 10 minutes in refrigerator. Bake for 7 minutes. Cool. Pour in the filling and return to the refrigerator for 30 minutes.

■ Heat jelly with wine until thinned. Slice fresh fruit: strawberries, raspberries and kiwi's are beautiful. Arrange on top of filling and brush with glaze.

Grilled Swordfish Fettuccine

SERVES 4-6

2 T Butter, melted
1 ½ lbs Swordfish
4 T Butter
¼ C Onions, chopped
2 Shallots, minced
½ C Celery, chopped
½ C Red pepper, sliced
½ C Summer squash, sliced
½ C Mushrooms, sliced
2 Tomatoes, seeded and chopped
12 oz Spinach fettuccine
¼ C Chardonnay
2 T Fresh basil, chopped
½ C Fresh Parmesan, grated
Salt and pepper
2 T Fresh lemon juice

Brush swordfish with melted butter and grill 10 minutes per inch of thickness. In a large skillet, sauté onions, shallots, vegetables and tomatoes in butter until just tender. Cook pasta until just tender and rinse. Chop the swordfish into 1" chunks and mix with vegetables and fettuccine. Add wine and basil and simmer for 2 minutes. Toss with Parmesan and adjust seasonings to taste. Sprinkle with lemon juice before serving.

Wine Suggestion: Chateau St. Jean, Fumé Blanc, La Petite Etiole.

Seafood Puffs

AN APPETIZER SERVING 4-6

FILLING
1 Clove garlic, minced
¼ C Green onions, chopped
¼ C Mushrooms, chopped
1 T Butter
½ lb Crab, cooked and chopped
½ lb Baby shrimp, cooked and chopped
12 oz Cream cheese
1 T Dry sherry
1 t Dill weed, dry
1 t Dijon mustard
Salt, pepper to taste
Egg White

PASTRY
½ Package puff pastry

SWEET HOT MUSTARD SAUCE
1 Egg
½ C Sugar
½ C Vinegar
½ C Dry mustard

Sauté the garlic and onions together in butter until tender. Add the mushrooms and sauté for a few more minutes. Whip the remaining filling ingredients together with the onion and mushroom mix. Cut puff pastry into 8 squares. Cut each square in half on the diagonal. Brush edges with egg white and place 2 teaspoons of seafood mixture in the center of the triangle. Fold in half, making a triangle and crimp the edges with a fork and seal with a brush of egg whites (if you bake them). Either bake in a preheated 375 degree oven for 15-20 minutes, or deep fry at 360 degrees for approximately 5 minutes.

■ Make the mustard sauce: beat the egg and add sugar. Add vinegar and dry mustard and mix fiercely. Heat in a double boiler, stirring constantly until thick. Serve the mustard sauce room temperature with the hot puffs.

Wine Suggestion: Silverado, Chardonnay.

High Alpine Restaurant

UPON ENTERING THE HIGH ALPINE RESTAURANT, YOU may perceive it to be like any mountain restaurant—a gift shop, a bar and a cafeteria line. But after you've spent a few moments wandering around, you'll realize it's not quite like any restaurant you've ever visited. Hanging on the main level is a windsurfer. Go one level up and you'll find a sailboat; a 16 foot Fireball complete with sails. Hanging upside down and looking like it may have just completed a loop, is a full-size, 50 foot wing span, sailplane. Look a bit further and you'll find a racing bike and a hang glider!

The owners of this museum-like mountain restaurant are George and Gwyn Gordon. Having run the Highlands Merry-Go-Round and Base Restaurants for six years, the Gordons moved over to Snowmass in 1979. Their philosophy and the reason for their success is, "it must be the best!" They strive for perfection in everything they do and it shows.

The cafeteria serves nutritious, wholesome meals. Some examples of their fare include: Shrimp and Wild Rice Salad, Chicken Brunswick Stew and Fresh Teriyaki Burgers. Their desserts, on the other hand, are mouth watering, naughty delights—some healthy, and some simply decadent. Try their carrot cake, chocolate Amaretto cheesecake, Bavarian apple torte, chocolate nougat bars or bread pudding with brandy sauce.

The employees at High Alpine are a cheerful, lively bunch. There's a definite camaraderie amongst them. The Gordons explain, "Our employees are the best in the valley. Most have just graduated from college or are taking a year off from grad school. They have decided they want to have the most fun year of their lives. They play and ski really hard and also bring the same enthusiasm for life to work with them. We really enjoy working with them!"

This personal enthusiasm, the food and the exciting atmosphere make High Alpine a definite place to stop for breakfast or lunch while skiing Snowmass.

Alpine Potatoes

Parboil, then thinly slice potatoes. Sauté vegetables with potatoes until tender. Blend in cream cheese, top with grated cheeses and place under broiler for 3 minutes. Garnish with parsley.

SERVES 2

3 Large red potatoes
3 T Butter
2 T Scallions, chopped
2 T Zucchini, chopped
2 T Mushrooms, chopped
2 T Tomatoes, chopped
¼ C Boursin herb cream cheese
½ C Grated Monterey Jack cheese
½ C Grated cheddar cheese
1 T Parsley, chopped

Scallop Fettuccine

SERVES 4

¼ C Butter
1 Clove garlic, minced
½ C Green onions,
    chopped
½ C Carrots, julienned
½ C Zucchini,
    julienned
½ C Mushrooms, sliced
¾ lb Bay scallops
1 lb Fettuccine
¾ C Heavy cream
1 C Fresh Parmesan
    cheese, grated
1 T Fresh basil, chopped
½ t Lemon juice
1 T Fresh parsley,
    chopped
Salt and white pepper to
    taste
Lemon wedges and fresh
    Parmesan (garnish)

In a large sauté pan, sauté the garlic and green onions in butter until tender. Add the next 4 ingredients and sauté for a few minutes more. Cook the fettuccine al dente according to directions. Toss with scallop mixture and add the cream and Parmesan. Add the basil, parsley and lemon juice. Cook until the cream thickens. Season to taste with salt and pepper. Serve immediately with lemon wedges and grated Parmesan.

Wine Suggestion: McDowell, Chardonnay.

Strawberry Mousse

SERVES 8

2 C Fresh strawberries
1 t Gelatin
2 T Water
⅜ C Sugar
1 ½ C Whip cream
1 t Vanilla
1 T Grand Marnier
Whip cream
Strawberries

Purée strawberries, then sieve to remove seeds. Sprinkle gelatin over cold water and let stand 5 minutes. Measure ¾ cup of purée and mix with sugar. When gelatin has softened, set over low heat, swirling to dissolve. Stir in purée quickly. Beat whip cream to soft peak stage. Fold in vanilla and Grand Marnier. Pour into eight 8-ounce parfait glasses and chill. Serve with a dollop of whip cream and garnish with strawberries.

Krabloonik

I F IT'S ADVENTURE AND ROMANCE YOU'RE SEEKING, Krabloonik is where you'll find it. It all began when Dan MacEachen took over the enormous task of training and taking care of Stuart Mace's Husky dogs. After an apprenticeship with Mace, MacEachen found a new home for the dogs near the slopes of the Snowmass ski area.

The dogs are born and bred for running and MacEachen trains them to pull dog sleds. The kennel hosts over 300 Huskies who willingly take people on two hour rides through the pristine wilderness. The happy howls of these special canines delight Snowmass skiers daily.

MacEachen knew the dogs alone wouldn't make ends meet, so he built a rustic log cabin restaurant to supplement his income. The idea was to be unique in this most unusual setting. They serve many items not found anywhere in this area—specifically wild game and game birds. Their Head Chef, Alan Fried, prepares classic French sauces that he embellishes with fresh herbs and spices. Manager Bill Dinsmoor explains, "We take advantage of using fresh ingredients. We grow our own herbs and use fresh fruits for sauces and desserts." The menu changes nightly with imaginative and harmonious combinations. They offer 4-6 wild game items each evening. Not many experience the opportunity to try wild boar, moose, elk or caribou. Game birds are popular with such favorites as pheasant, duck and quail prepared in an appealing manner. For those not "wild" about game, you can choose from an array of fresh fish which the kitchen handles with a delicate touch. Beef entrées are also available. Dinsmoor told me the most popular dish is caribou. "It has a naturally sweet flavor and is more delicate than beef."

The desserts are presented on a tray after the meal, and not many can pass up these tempting delights.

The wine list is carefully selected by Dinsmoor with over 200 wines, mostly from California. He changes the list twice a year and keeps it moderately priced. He enjoys making suggestions to customers who are often baffled by their entrée choice.

Dinsmoor notes about their patrons, "We really enjoy the people who dine with us. We catch them in new territory. By the time they've walked down our long stairway, seen the dogs and feasted their eyes on our splendid view of Mt. Daly, they're usually hooked! They're willing to explore and experiment in this unpretentious environment."

Most people inquire about the name, Krabloonik. MacEachen named the restaurant after his first lead dog. The term in Alaskan means, "Big Eye Brows." MacEachen has put his work to the ultimate test and has participated in the famous Iditarod race twice. It's a grueling 1,200 mile dog sled race from Anchorage to Nome, Alaska. The restaurant exhibits many photographs of this daring, exciting endeavor.

Pear Conserve

MAKES 2 GALLONS

1 Gallon pear purée
  (pulp)
1 C Lemon juice
1 ½ C Brandy
2 C Pecan pieces,
  chopped
1 ½ C Currants
1 ½ C Pectin
10 C Sugar
1 Case small Mason
  canning jars

Combine all ingredients except sugar. Bring to preboil. Add sugar and bring to rolling boil. Stir to prevent scorching. Boil for 5 minutes. Can or freeze.

White Chocolate Grand Marnier Mousse

Melt chocolate with water and Grand Marnier. Whisk until smooth. Let cool. Whip the cream until soft peaks form. Fold whipped cream into chocolate mixture. Place into individual serving glasses and refrigerate, covered.

SERVES 12

1   lb, 11 ounces White
    chocolate
½ C Water
¾ C Grand Marnier
4 ½ C Whipped cream

Wild Mushroom Soup

MAKES 12 CUPS

2 C Dried wild
   mushrooms (soaked),
   or 2 cups fresh wild
   mushrooms
1 Large onion
1 C Red wine
1 Pint buttermilk
12 oz Sour cream
4 oz Plain yogurt
2 C Rich beef stock
   (Magi concentrate
   will work)
½ C Cornstarch
1½ Qt Water
Garlic to taste
Salt and pepper to taste

Strain liquid and save from dried mushrooms. Purée mushrooms and onion. Add strained liquid and all other ingredients except for cornstarch and save some sour cream for garnish. Bring to low boil. Dissolve cornstarch in lukewarm water, then whisk into soup. Stir so it doesn't stick and scorch. Cook 3-5 minutes (or longer) until thickened. Garnish with dollop of sour cream!

The kicker: a bowl of this soup combined with a loaf of warm, homemade bread and a lovely salad makes a wonderful meal.

Wine Suggestion: Fumé Blanc. Chateau St. Jean, La Petite Etoile.

The Main Buttermilk Restaurant

I**T'S YOUR FIRST DAY SKIING. YOU'RE HEADED OUT TO** Buttermilk Mountain because you heard it's a haven for rank beginners. And that's exactly what you are!

You forgot your goggles, gloves and scarf rushing out the door. A good cup of coffee would ease your ever-present nervousness.

You've come to the right spot. Located at the base of this non-threatening mountain is the Main Buttermilk Restaurant. They have a well-stocked gift shop, a bar with a cheerful bartenderess named Ellyn and a cafeteria which serves breakfast, lunch and snacks. Try Eggs Buttermilk, a variation of Eggs Benedict. It's the perfect choice for skiers who crave early-morning nourishment. They also serve homemade muffins, delicious cinnamon rolls, and great hot coffee.

Lunch features the standard fare of burgers and hot dogs, but they also cater to those who are more health conscious. They have an extensive salad bar and sandwiches to order. Salmon with cream cheese on a croissant is a favorite. There is always a daily special. Look for satisfying, ethnic creations such as: Mexican, Oriental, West Indies or Italian. Finish the meal with one of their scrumptious, homemade desserts.

Peter and Jan Wirth are the proprietors of this establishment. Peter was born and raised in Aspen. His parents, Paul and Hannah, ran the Sundeck Restaurant on the top of Aspen Mountain from 1952-1966. Peter has many fond memories of his early years spent living on top of a ski mountain. He also recalls many cold mornings skiing to school!

After a short retirement, the Wirths were persuaded to run the Sam's Knob Restaurant on the newly-opened Snowmass Mountain. Peter and Jan worked at "The Knob" to help out, and in doing so, gained the expertise for running a restaurant of their own. Eventually, this energetic couple transferred to Main Buttermilk and enjoy carrying on the tradition of a family-run restaurant.

Chocolate Silk Pie

CRUST
1 ¼ C Graham cracker
    crumbs
¼ C Sugar
¼ C Softened butter

FILLING
1 Stick softened butter
3 Eggs
2 ½ Squares semi-sweet
    chocolate, melted

GARNISH
½ pt Whipping cream

Make crust: mix together all 3 ingredients. Pour into 9" pie plate and press firmly. Bake at 375 degrees for 8 minutes. Cool.
■ Make filling: combine all 3 ingredients in a blender. Blend until smooth, at least 2 minutes. Add 1 teaspoon of vanilla if desired. Pour into graham cracker crust. Cover and refrigerate. Whip cream until quite stiff. Garnish pie by mounding piles of whipped cream along the outer edge of the pie. Pie can be garnished with either chocolate or white chocolate curls if desired.

The kicker: if you really want to indulge yourself and your guests, serve a dessert wine with this pie. We suggest a Sauternes—Comtesse Durieu De Lacarelle.

Cream of Carrot Soup

SERVES 6

5   C Homemade
    chicken stock
2   C Carrots, diced
1/2 C Onion, diced
1/2 C Flour
4   oz Butter
1   Quart heavy cream
2   Bay leaves
White pepper

Sauté onions and carrots in a large soup pot. Add chicken stock and bring to a boil. Whisk together flour and butter in a separate pan. Blend this roux into the chicken stock. Bring back to a boil and add heavy cream (use as much or as little as you prefer until you reach desired thickness). Season to taste. If a smoother soup is desired, put the soup through a food mill. Serve immediately.

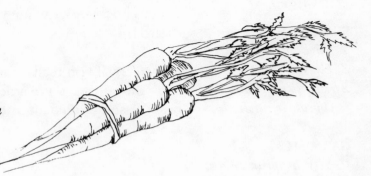

Smoked Turkey Salad

Combine salad ingredients. Make sherried mayonnaise: combine first 4 ingredients in food processor. Process for 1 minute. Slowly dribble in oil until it is all mixed in. Scrape down the food bowl and season to taste with salt and pepper. Toss the salad with this mayonnaise.

Wine Suggestion: Sonoma Cutrer, Chardonnay.

SERVES 4

SALAD
1 ½ lbs Smoked turkey,
    cut into 2" julienne
    strips
¾ lbs Jarlsberg cheese,
    cut into 2" julienne
    strips
1 C Red or green
    seedless grapes, halved
1 C Celery, diced
1 C Snow peas
½ C Pecans, chopped
¼ C Black olives, sliced

SHERRIED MAYONNAISE
1 Whole egg
2 Egg yolks
1 T Dijon mustard
¼ C Sherry vinegar
2 C Vegetable oil
Salt and pepper

The Merry-Go-Round
Restaurant

THE MERRY-GO-ROUND WAS NAMED BY HIGHLANDS'
owner, Whip Jones. The significance being that it is located at
the center of the ski area and all activity flows around it.
George Schermerhorn and Robert Cronenberg have co-owned the
restaurant since 1982. They brought Gretl Uhl with them as their food
consultant. Gretl had just retired from her tiny restaurant on Aspen
Mountain and wanted to pass on her knowledge to others. Schermerhorn and Cronenberg benefited from this arrangement because Gretl
had such a wonderful reputation and skiers missed her style of cooking.

Gretl's strudl was once again baking and emitting those wondrous
aromas—to the enjoyment of hundreds of skiers daily. She taught these
two young owners how to make strudl her way—only using the best ingredients and peeling and coring the apples by hand. They sell frozen
strudl to anyone on request. It comes with baking instructions so that
people can now enjoy this famous dessert at home!

Many of the dishes served at the Merry-Go-Round are Gretl's recipes,
but each year, as Schermerhorn and Cronenberg felt more confident,
they have expanded and added many of their own creations, which have
turned out to be successes in their own right.

The appearance of their cafeteria line looks as appealing as Gretl's
did—one dish looks better than the next. Perhaps it's because of this
extra care and labor-intensive preparation that elicits constant praises
from hungry skiers. The desserts, which are presented first, are impos-
sible to pass up. In addition to the strudl, the most popular items are
Maui rum cake (it's authentic!), trifle and cream puffs. Their creative and
colorful salads change often depending on fresh produce. Favorites are:
pasta salad, tomatoes stuffed with shrimp and Crab Louis, stuffed avo-

cado and Gretl's spinach salad. There are two soups made fresh daily, chili, ratatouille, Gretl's secret sauerkraut, and, of course, burgers and fresh sandwiches. An innovative daily special is featured for variety, and a full wine list is offered for accompaniment.

Schermerhorn and Cronenberg also run the Cloud 9 restaurant. It's actually a small and intimate mountain hut located at the summit of the Cloud 9 chairlift. They serve the same delicious fare on a smaller basis and feature an outdoor grill. The main attraction is the Ski Patrol exhibition. To the amazement of everyone (weather permitting), Ski Patrolmen dazzle you in daredevil jumps over the deck of the restaurant! It's definitely a show not to be missed.

It's no small task to run two mountain restaurants. The owners' philosophy shows in everything they do. They don't think cafeteria food has to be dull, conversely, it can be very exciting. Schermerhorn explains, "We know that you can feed 2,000 people the same food you might serve 20. We're not limited in scope and we're not afraid to try new things. You just need to be willing to take a chance."

Ratatouille

SERVES 8-10

6 Garlic gloves, crushed
4 Medium onions, chop
  1, quarter the others
1 Red pepper, julienne
1 Green pepper,
  julienne
1 Large eggplant, diced
1 Green zucchini, sliced
1 Yellow zucchini,
  sliced
1 Large can plum
  tomatoes (Progresso)
1 Medium can tomato
  sauce (Progresso)
½ C Olive oil
3 T basil
Salt and pepper
Freshly grated
  Parmesan cheese

Be sure to use a good brand of canned tomato products (we recommend Progresso). Place olive oil in a large stock pot, add onions and sauté until transparent. Add garlic and stir for 30 seconds, remove from heat. Add all vegetables, basil, salt and pepper. Pour canned tomatoes and tomato sauce over. Simmer covered over low heat, stir occasionally. Don't overcook. Vegetables should be firm. If you wish to reduce liquid, simmer uncovered. Serve hot or cold topped with Parmesan cheese. May be used as a side dish or as an entrée with rice or pasta.

Wine Suggestion: Sebastiani, Cabernet Sauvignon.

Tomatoes Stuffed with Shrimp and Crab Louis

SERVES 8-10

Hollow out tomatoes. Save insides for soup (or whatever). Combine all ingredients except crab and shrimp and whisk together. In a separate bowl, combine shrimp and crab, broken up. Pour sauce over all and toss. Stuff tomatoes with mixture. Place on serving plates with lettuce and garnish with lemon wedges. Serve with melba toast or crisp French bread. Can be prepared several hours ahead and refrigerated.

Wine Suggestion: Estrella, Chardonnay.

8-10 Large ripe tomatoes
2 C Popcorn shrimp (200-300 ct) or larger, cooked
1 C Crab meat, cleaned and cooked
¾ C Mayonnaise, or to taste
1 T Lemon juice
½ t Worcestershire
Dash Tabasco
2 T Heavy cream
Dash cayenne
Salt and pepper

The Pine Creek Cookhouse

NESTLED HIGH ABOVE ASPEN, IN THE EXQUISITE Ashcroft Valley, is a quaint Alpine restaurant. The Pine Creek Cookhouse is situated in the heart of the Ashcroft Ski Touring area. Dine for lunch and dinner on Hungarian and European cuisine with the most breathtaking view of the Elk Mountain range. Winter access to the Cookhouse is either by cross-country skiing or by horse-drawn sleigh.

An evening at the Cookhouse is a wonderful experience. Ski in with miners' headlamps for a fantastic dinner "away from it all." It's relaxing and fun. After a chilly ski, warm up with a hot drink by the pot belly stove and enjoy Krisi's Hungarian cheese dip and a glass of wine. Dinners feature predominately French cuisine. The menu changes often depending on the chef's whims and the availability of fresh ingredients.

Ashcroft Ski Touring offers 30 kilometers of set cross-country ski tracks in this pristine valley. Stop for a nutritious, wholesome lunch at the Cookhouse. There are hearty winter soups, homemade breads, an unusual salad bar (with Tabouli, Quinoa, pasta salads, etc.), sandwiches, spinach crêpes and a daily hot pasta.

Summer at Ashcroft holds its own beauty. You can drive or bike from Aspen, or horseback ride from a nearby ranch.

Lunch and dinner are once again served. The lunch menu is basically the same with cold salads and iced cherry soup to complement the warm days. For dinner, fish, chicken and duck are prepared on a mesquite grill.

Formerly owned by Ruthie and Ted Ryan, the land is now owned by filmmaker, John Wilcox. Greg and Krisi Mace ran the ski touring area and the restaurant for 12 years. After Greg Mace's tragic death in a climbing accident, Krisi is once again the magic force behind the Pine Creek Cookhouse's success.

Krisi's love of the area, her delicious creative Hungarian cooking and her desire to have others share in this mountain experience, make the Pine Creek Cookhouse an idyllic place to dine.

Korozott (Hungarian Cheese Spread)

Bring cream cheese to room temperature. Melt butter. Put all ingredients into Cuisinart and blend well. Serve with cocktail bread or vegetables.

MAKES 2 CUPS

1 lb Cream cheese
1/3 lb Butter
3/4 C Sour cream
1/3 C Green onions, chopped
1 T Hungarian paprika

1 T Caraway seeds
1 T Dijon mustard
1/2 lb Cottage cheese
1 T Anchovy paste
1 T Capers

Krisi's Brownies with Hot Fudge Sauce

MAKES 24

BROWNIES

1 Stick plus 3 Tablespoons Butter
2 oz Semi-sweet chocolate
4 oz Unsweetened chocolate
1 C Brown sugar, tightly packed
1 C Granulated sugar
1 ½ t Vanilla
1 ½ C Flour
1 t Salt
2 t Baking powder
4 Eggs
½ C Chopped nuts (your choice, we use almonds)

Preheat oven to 350 degrees. Use a 9" X 13" pan. Make brownies: in a heavy medium sized saucepan, melt butter and chocolates over low heat, stirring occasionally. When all are melted, remove from heat and stir in sugars and vanilla. Add flour, salt and baking powder and mix well. Then add the eggs, stirring briefly after each addition. Sprinkle top with chopped nuts. Bake 25-30 minutes, more for a double batch. Toothpick should come out dry.

■ Make sauce: in a small saucepan, melt butter. Remove from heat, add cocoa, whisk until smooth. Stir in chocolate, sugar and evaporated milk or whipping cream. Bring to boil over medium heat stirring constantly. Remove from heat. Stir in salt, cool and stir in vanilla.

■ Serve brownies with hot fudge sauce and whipped cream!

HOT FUDGE SAUCE

5 T Butter
¼ C Cocoa powder
2 Squares unsweetened chocolate
¾ C Granulated sugar
⅔ C Whipping cream or evaporated milk
Pinch salt
1 t Vanilla

Krisi's Specialty Muffins

MAKES 12 MUFFINS

2 ½ C Flour (white or whole wheat)
1 T Baking powder
½ t Salt
½ C Honey
½ C Walnuts, chopped
1 ½ t Cinnamon
1 Egg
¼ C Safflower oil
1 C Buttermilk
1 t Vanilla
¼ t Cloves, ground
3-4 T Apricot jam or ½ cup fresh fruit

Preheat oven to 400 degrees. Grease well 12 muffin pan cups. Into bowl, sift flour, baking powder and salt. Add walnuts, cloves and cinnamon. In a separate bowl, beat egg until frothy. Stir in buttermilk, oil, honey, vanilla and jam or fruit. Mix well. Make small well in flour mixture, pour in milk mixture all at once. Stir quickly and lightly—don't beat, just mix and stir. Quickly fill muffin cups two thirds full. Bake 25 minutes or until toothpick comes out clean. Serve hot!

Spenot Palacsinta (Spinach Crêpes)

SERVES 6

CRÊPE BATTER
4 Eggs
1 C Milk
½ C White flour
½ C Whole wheat flour
2 T Oil
1 C Club soda water

SPINACH FILLING
4 T Margarine
¼ C Green onions,
   chopped
1 t Hungarian paprika
   (found in specialty
   stores)
Pinch garlic powder
¼ t White pepper
¼ C Flour
1 C Chicken broth
½ C Milk
1 C Mushrooms,
   chopped
½ C Cheddar cheese,
   shredded

2 C Cooked spinach,
   chopped
Pinch nutmeg
1 T Worcestershire
   sauce

TOPPING
1 C Sour Cream
1 C Buttermilk
Fresh Parmesan cheese,
   grated

To make crêpes: put flour and milk into a large bowl and whisk until very smooth. Add oil, eggs and mix well. Add soda water and stir. Refrigerate overnight. Make crêpes in any standard crêpe or omelette pan.

■ To make filling: melt margarine in small saucepan, sauté green onions, add paprika, garlic and pepper. Whisk in flour and blend thoroughly. Remove from heat and whisk in chicken broth and milk. Cool, stirring constantly, until mixture is smooth. Add mushrooms and cheese. Heat and stir until cheese is melted. Add spinach, nutmeg and worcestershire sauce. Stir. Spoon filling into crêpes and wrap around.

■ To make topping: whisk sour cream and buttermilk together. Spoon 3 or 4 tablespoons on each crêpe. Sprinkle with fresh Parmesan and place under broiler until Parmesan melts.

Wine Suggestion: Badacsoni Kéknyelï (a Hungarian Chenin Blanc!).

Les Chefs D'Aspen

THIS UNIQUE SHOP, ON THE BUSY CORNER OF COOPER and Hunter Streets, is a combination of retail cookware and gift items, gourmet food items, gourmet-to-go food shop, patio for sampling these delicacies and a kitchen for various cooking classes. It's "one-stop shopping." You can purchase the equipment, many of the ingredients, recipes and the know-how to go home and cook a fabulous meal. Or, you can choose from any number of their packaged gourmet dishes to take home, put in the microwave or oven, and have for dinner.

Les Chefs is a fun shop, whether you're looking to buy a cookbook, a gift for a special occasion or an espresso coffee machine. The staff, headed up by Sally Jo Mullen, who runs this entire operation, is always helpful and cheery. If you love kitchen shops, a visit to Les Chefs is a must.

The back of the shop is a wonderland of culinary delights. Michael McHugh, the Head Chef, offers both catering and gourmet-to-go.

He caters small or large affairs. Many people, both groups and families, come to Aspen and simply don't want to cook. Michael and his crew can take care of their needs. Wouldn't you love to come home from a hard day on the slopes and sit down to this meal: Chinese noodles with shrimp and Sezchuan sausage in a miso broth with fresh mint and cilantro, seven greens with beer mustard vinaigrette, grilled chicken with black chantrelle, trumpet and oyster mushrooms in a port sauce with fresh sage, and for dessert, fresh fruit and chocolate macadamia-nut cookies?

Michael compares cooking to an artist at his canvas, "I don't always know what I'm going to make until I'm in front of the stove. I create as I go with what's available and with what's fresh."

If, on the other hand, you've skied all day and want something quick and easy, yet not "Swansons," try their gourmet-to-go. "It's convenient cuisine, restaurant-quality dishes ready to take home and cook quickly." They sell entrées, fresh pastas and sauces. You can purchase cheeses, breads, salads and desserts. They will also do any special order. It's a great way for a family to eat well, without the hassles of always going to a restaurant.

Les Chefs has wonderful cooking classes throughout the winter and summer. They offer a variety of fun and informative classes with both local and internationally-known guest chefs.

They are working to become an accredited school. Sally explains, "We get letters from all over the country asking about our classes. Wouldn't this be the perfect place to receive accreditation?" Sally and Michael agree that Aspen is becoming more and more aware of food and cooking as an art form. And they would like to create a place where the culinary arts can flourish.

Brownies of Death

MAKES 24

½ C Butter

4 oz Semi-sweet chocolate

4 Eggs, room temperature

½ t Salt

2 C Sugar

1 T Espresso powder (found in some supermarkets or specialty shops)

1 C All-purpose flour, sifted

1 C White chocolate chips (found in specialty shops)

Melt butter and chocolate. Mix in espresso powder to dissolve. Let mixture cool. Beat eggs and salt until foamy and add sugar gradually. Combine cooled chocolate mixture with eggs and sugar. Fold in flour and chocolate chips. Bake in greased 9" X 13" pan for approximately 25 minutes at 350 degrees. When cool, cut and dust with confectioners sugar. Yummy!

Lasagna Al Pesto

SERVES 6

PESTO SAUCE
1 C Fresh basil
½ C Walnuts
2 Small cloves garlic
½ C Olive oil
½ C Fresh Parmesan
   cheese

FILLING
1 lb Fresh spinach
1 C Onion, minced
3 T Olive oil
Salt and pepper to taste
½ C Parmesan cheese,
   grated
4 C Ricotta cheese
20-24 Green lasagna
   noodles
1 lb Mozzarella cheese,
   thin slices or grated
¼ lb Sunflower seeds
   (optional)

Make pesto sauce: combine basil, garlic and walnuts in bowl, blender or food processor and chop. Leave motor running and add the olive oil in a slow, steady stream. Shut motor off, add the cheese, pinch of salt and a liberal grinding of pepper. Process briefly to combine ingredients. Scrape out into bowl and cover until ready to use.

■ Make the filling: clean spinach and chop fine in food processor or blender. Sauté onions in 2 tablespoons of olive oil, stir in raw spinach with hot onions. Transfer to large bowl. Add ½ cup Parmesan cheese, pesto, ricotta and sunflower seeds (if desired) and grind in pepper. Mix thoroughly with spoon. Cook pasta (dente), drain and drizzle with remaining olive oil. Layer in 9" X 13" pan starting with noodles, filling, Mozzarella and ending with noodles. Sprinkle with Parmesan cheese and drizzle with olive oil. Cover with foil and bake at 350 degrees for 35-40 minutes.

Wine Suggestion: Ruffino, Chianti Reserve 1978.

Sweet Roasted Peppers

SERVES 6-8

8 Red and yellow
   peppers, roasted and
   peeled
½ C Extra virgin olive
   oil
Salt and pepper, added
   to oil
10-12 Fresh basil leaves,
   julienned in strips

Roast peppers over open flame turning occasionally until completely blackened. Cool peppers for handling. Cut off both ends of peppers and remove core. Lie flat on board to scrape off blackened peeling. Wash gently under cool water to remove any remaining blackened peeling. Drain on towel until dry. Quarter peppers, place on plate or tray, overlapping edges. Drizzle oil over top and garnish with basil strips. Refrigerate and serve.

Serving Suggestions: a colorful and tasty accompaniment with most entrées, salads and sandwiches.

Tortellini Salad with Feta Cheese

SERVES 6

½ C Olive oil
¼ C White wine
   vinegar
¼ C Green onion,
   chopped
3 Small cloves garlic,
   chopped
1 T Dried basil,
   crumbled
1 t Dried dill,
   crumbled
2 12 ounce Packages
   stuffed tortellini
   (cook according to
   directions)
1 Can artichoke hearts,
   drained and
   quartered
1 Large tomato,
   chopped
½ C Feta cheese,
   crumbled
½ C Black olives,
   chopped
½ C Walnuts, chopped

Whisk oil and vinegar in small bowl. Add onion, garlic, basil, dill and mix well. Combine remaining ingredients in large bowl. Pour dressing over and toss gently. Refrigerate 8-10 hours before serving.

Wine Suggestion: Frog's Leap, Chardonnay.

Marika's Catering

IMAGINE A GREEK FEAST CATERED IN YOUR HOME. IMAGINE being entertained by belly dancers while sipping Greek wine and devouring moussaka, spanikopita and Greek salad.

Eleni Theos Stalter can cater just about any party, but her Greek cooking and entertaining are her specialties. She is of Greek heritage and uses many of her grandmother's recipes. She has always loved to cook.

Upon moving to Aspen, she owned a Greek restaurant for three years. She felt it was "time for Aspen to educate its palate with a more varied, ethnic cuisine."

Her Greek favorites include: Dolmathaikia, Tabouli, Lemon Chicken, Tiropita and Taramosalata. She also has her own line of mouth-watering desserts. People adore her chocolate apricot baklava, her chocolate pecan torte and her truffles!

Eleni's Spanikopita

SERVES 12

9 *Large eggs, beat until fluffy*

¾ *lb Feta cheese, crumbled*

1 *Medium onion, diced*

2 *10 oz Packages, frozen, chopped spinach, thawed and drained well through cheesecloth*

1 *T Pepper*

1 *T Dill weed, dried, or 2 T fresh*

1 *lb Butter or margarine, unsalted*

1 *lb Filo leaves, thawed*

Use a 9 ½" X 13" pan, stainless or enameled. In a large bowl, mix together the eggs, feta cheese, onion, pepper and dill weed. Add spinach. Melt butter. Open package of filo. Lay flat on large work surface next to baking pan. Butter bottom and sides of pan with a soft pastry brush. Take 2 sheets of filo, lay in pan, butter bottom and sides of top sheet. Repeat this process 3 more times until you've used 8 sheets total, (to make the bottom layer). Be generous with your butter.

■ Now make a "pocket" of filo. Take 2 sheets at a time and place around the pan—meeting half-way in pan so it looks similar to this diagram.

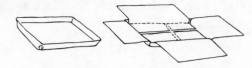

■ Work quickly. Keep filo covered with a lightly dampened cloth. Use 8 sheets for this part. Butter sheets both inside and outside pan (about ½" deep). Pour filling into pocket, spreading evenly. Fold in sides of filo, covering the filling. Butter. Add 6 more layers of filo, 2 sheets at a time, buttering between each layer. Trim edges neatly to pan. Cut layers into 12 equal pieces, then score each piece diagonally. For appetizer pieces, cut each piece with 2 diagonals to make 4 small triangles. Bake 1 hour at 375 degrees or 350 degrees below 5,000 feet. You must cut before baking! You can freeze baked or unbaked.

Wine Suggestion: Roditys, a Greek Rosé wine.

Moussaka

SERVES 12

3-4 Medium eggplants
2 lbs Ground lamb or
 beef or both
1 Medium onion,
 chopped
1 Clove garlic, minced
½ t Nutmeg
¼ t Cinnamon
½ t Fine herbes
2 T Fresh parsley,
 chopped
1 8 oz Can tomato
 sauce
½ C Red wine
½ C Water
Olive oil
¾ C Fresh Parmesan
 cheese, grated
4 C Bechamel sauce
 (recipe follows)

Peel and slice eggplant lengthwise into ½" slices; salt well on both sides; set aside for 20-30 minutes. Prepare meat sauce (kimá): sauté meat with salt and pepper, onion and garlic. When evenly browned, drain off most of the fat. Add next 7 ingredients. Stir to mix well, return to burner, bring to a boil and simmer for 20 minutes. While kimá is simmering, wash and drain eggplant in cold water. Pat dry with paper towel and begin to fry in olive oil. Drain each layer on paper towels. You can deep fry eggplant to a golden brown. The best flavor is to deep fry about 2 minutes on each side.

■ Use a greased 9 ½" X 13" pan (not aluminum). Place a layer of eggplant, filling in spaces as best you can (like a jigsaw puzzle); top with meat mixture, sprinkle with grated cheese; top with another layer of eggplant, sprinkle with grated cheese and cover with bechamel sauce. Top lavishly with grated cheese. Bake 1 hour at 350 degrees or 375 degrees over 5,000 feet. Moussaka must cool at least one hour before serving.

Bechamel Sauce

Scant ½ cup flour
½ C Margarine
4 C Milk
¼ t Nutmeg
¼ C Grated cheese
(Romano or
Parmesan)
¼ t White pepper
3 Egg yolks

Heat milk to very hot, not boiling. Melt margarine with flour in large saucepan, stir with whisk until smooth. Gradually add milk, stirring constantly until it thickens. Remove from heat. Add next 3 ingredients. Whisk in egg yolks and pour over moussaka. You can freeze moussaka, either baked or unbaked. You can substitute zucchini or potatoes for eggplant.

The kicker: this is very time consuming, but well worth the effort!

Wine Suggestion: Danielis 1979, a dry red Greek wine.

Taramosalata à la Marika's

AN APPETIZER. MAKES 3 CUPS.

2 *Medium potatoes*
¼-⅓ *C Milk*
3 *T Tarama roe (found in specialty or Greek stores)*
3 *T Onion, finely chopped*
2 *C Virgin olive oil, preferably Greek or French*
3 *T Fresh lemon juice*

Boil potatoes. When *well* cooked, put in food processor with milk—they must be very creamy, almost runny. Add tarama and onion with processor running continuously. Begin adding olive oil in a slow, steady stream. The mixture will begin to thicken. Continue to add olive oil until you've used approximately 1 ½ cups. Add lemon juice, let mix for 1 minute, then add remaining olive oil. Taste—the mixture may need a little more lemon juice.

■ Mixture is very thick and creamy. Delicious served with warm bread, melba toast, a stuffing for cucumbers or tomatoes, etc. Will keep in refrigerator 10 days-2 weeks.

Tsaziki Sauce

4 *lb Thick yogurt (Mountain High)*
3 *Large cucumbers*
7 *Cloves garlic*
1 *T Olive oil*
2 *t Wine vinegar*

Purée cucumbers in food processor, drain through cheesecloth. Peel garlic. Place 1 cup yogurt in a blender. Add garlic, olive oil, vinegar and purée about 2 minutes. Add all ingredients together and mix well. Let stand 2-3 hours to allow flavors to blend. Wonderful sauce for meat and fish. Excellent as a dip for crudités, bread, stuffed grape leaves, salad dressing, etc.

■ Keeps about 2 weeks. Can be doubled or halved, depending on need.

Peter O'Grady's Creative Catering

I T'S NOT UNCOMMON. PETER O'GRADY CAME TO ASPEN AS A ski bum and decided to stay. However, O'Grady is one of the lucky ones—he started his own catering business and was able to survive in a town where the "ski bum" is a term of the past.

He gained experience at Shannon's Galley, 13 years ago, where he apprenticed under Michael Shannon. He soon became their head chef and ran the kitchen. After various and assorted jobs, O'Grady, along with Julie Murad, started their own catering business. Their timing was perfect. It was during a period when several caterers quit. Julie and Peter filled a niche in Aspen for catering with a creative touch.

"We started out catering mostly private dinner parties until we built up a reputation." From there, O'Grady explains, "we started catering large events like the Aspen Club Celebrity Tennis Tournament, parties for the various arts and culture groups and large corporate functions." O'Grady bought out his partner and is now on his own. "Catering is a real challenge for me. My clients expect me to create something really special." And that he does. His services run the gamut; he provides flower arranging, costumes, decorations, music, varied menus and wine suggestions.

He cooks with the freshest of everything that is available. He buys outstanding herbs and produce from a local grower. When asked what cuisine he prefers, O'Grady replies, "I have a French cooking background, which is the basis for everything I do, but I'm extremely flexible. You have to be in this business whether it be a down-home picnic, an intimate French dinner or a Mexican feast. There is always much research to be done to obtain the right look and the right taste of the cuisine for my clients. It's exciting to be given the chance to test myself constantly."

O'Grady's newest venture is food styling. Jill St. John contracted him in the summer of '86 when she decided to photograph her cookbook in Aspen. O'Grady describes food styling as, "the preparation of food for photographing." The project became quite a challenge and required much experimentation. He enjoyed it. Food styling is a realm O'Grady intends to pursue further.

He continues to read, travel and take classes in order to stay current in the food business. O'Grady says with a grin, "I feel like I've only just begun. So much more is open to me than before which is a function of being happy with my work."

Chicken Dijonnaise

SERVES 6

2 Shallots, chopped fine
1 Large clove garlic,
   chopped fine
2 T Unsalted butter
3 T Brandy
¾ C White wine
1 ½ T Dijon mustard
1 T Fresh tarragon,
   chopped
¼ t Garlic salt
1 t Fresh ground pepper
2 Shots Tabasco
3 C Beef stock
2 ½ lbs Boneless chicken
   breasts, skinless
6 T Heavy whipping
   cream
4 T Butter
2 T Cornstarch
1 T Water

Sauté shallots and garlic in 2 tablespoons butter until shallots are clear (approximately 5 minutes) on medium heat. Add brandy and white wine. Bring to a boil and reduce for 8 minutes. Add mustard, garlic salt, tarragon, black pepper and Tabasco. Stir well. Add beef stock and bring to a boil. Reduce heat to simmer and cook 20-30 minutes. While sauce is simmering, prepare the chicken.

■ In a heavy bottomed pot, place 4 tablespoons butter in pot and turn to low heat. While butter is melting, trim away any remaining fat, skin or cartilage from chicken breasts. Divide into breast halves if necessary. Pat breasts dry. Place into melted butter turning once to coat evenly. Cut a piece of foil large enough to cover the chicken but not to seal the pot. Place on top of chicken allowing a gap for steam to escape. Cook on very low heat, not allowing chicken to brown, for 15 minutes. Turn chicken and cook covered as before for 10 minutes. Chicken will be very moist. Remove to warm platter.

■ To the sauce, add heavy cream and bring to a boil. Reduce for 5 minutes. To make cornstarch mixture, add water to cornstarch and stir with fingers until smooth. Slowly add this mixture to sauce to thicken. To serve, pour sauce over chicken.

Wine Suggestion: Villa Mt. Eden 1984, Chardonnay.

Pear Baclava

SERVES 12

1 lb Filo dough, thawed
2 Sticks butter, melted
4 Fresh pears
4 oz Walnuts, chopped
  small
¼ C Brown sugar
2 oz Maple syrup
Cinnamon
Nutmeg
½ Lemon, squeezed
⅔ C Sugar
¼ C Water
2 oz Maple syrup

Thaw filo according to directions. Remove packet from box and unfold. Trim the filo to fit a 9" X 13" pan. Cover with a damp cloth.

■ Peel, quarter and core the pears. Slice each quarter across into thin slices. Toss pear slices in a bowl with lemon juice, maple syrup, cinnamon, nutmeg and walnuts. Set aside. Brush bottom and sides of baking dish lightly with melted butter. Place 1 sheet filo on bottom and brush the top lightly with butter. Add 6 more layers of filo brushing lightly with butter each layer. Spread pears over top of filo layers. Spread brown sugar over top of pears.

■ Add 6-8 more layers of filo and lightly brush with butter each time. Bake at 350 degrees for 30 minutes or until brown and puffy. Remove from oven and set aside. Combine sugar, water and maple syrup in a small saucepan and bring to a boil. Reduce heat and simmer for 10 minutes. Cut a diagonal crisscross pattern through the layers of filo spacing 1 ½". Pour syrup mixture over top and let stand for 30 minutes before serving.

Pesto Shrimp

AN APPETIZER SERVING 6

1 lb Medium shrimp
   (24 pieces), peeled
   and deveined
3 T Pesto sauce (see
   recipe from
   Pinocchio's)
6 oz Chèvre cheese
1 T Olive oil
24 Bamboo skewers

Toss the shrimp in pesto sauce. Refrigerate for at least 30 minutes. Preheat oven to 450 degrees. Skewer shrimp 1 or 2 per skewer depending on taste. Lightly oil a cookie sheet. Place skewered shrimp side by side on cookie sheet. Crumble cheese into small pieces and cover top of shrimp with cheese. Bake 15 minutes or until pink.

Bibb Salad with Lemon Vinaigrette

2 Medium heads of bibb
   lettuce
½ Lemon, squeezed and
   seeds removed
3 T Extra virgin olive
   oil
Fresh ground pepper
½ t Minced fresh thyme
2 Pinches salt

Rinse the bibb leaves and pat or spin dry. Lettuce can be stored in plastic bag with a paper towel and refrigerated for up to 2 hours. Pour oil into small bowl. Whisk lemon juice into oil with a fork. Add salt, thyme and pepper and rewhisk. Let stand at least 10 minutes before serving. Break leaves into desired size, toss with dressing and serve.

High Altitude and Low Altitude Cooking Conversions

These recipes have been prepared for high altitude (above 7,000 feet) cooking. However, contrary to popular belief, adjusting them to low altitude requires very little work. In fact many of the recipes in this book will work perfectly when cooked at sea level. Many of these recipes were tested both in Aspen and at lower elevations to prove this theory. Breads, cakes and muffins are the few exceptions. The following hints will allow you to be successful:

YEAST DOUGH: Increase the flour. Plan on 15 minutes longer to rise at lower altitudes.

CAKES AND QUICK BREADS: Increase each teaspoon of baking powder or soda by $1/4$ teaspoon and increase the sweetener by $1/8$ cup for each cup requested. Decrease liquids from 1 to 4 tablespoons per cup and lower the oven temperature 25 degrees.

MUFFINS: Increase sweetener and baking powder by a fourth.

On the other hand, if this is your first attempt at cooking at high altitude, you'll want to know the following information:

☐ The air is thinner which causes less pressure.

☐ Liquids boil at a lower temperatures than at sea level.

☐ If boiling anything, plan on a longer cooking time.

☐ Because the air is drier, plan on using extra liquids to prevent evaporation. Don't be surprised at how quickly yeast dough rises!

Abbreviations   C=cup   t=teaspoon   T=tablespoon   oz=ounce

Introduction

"Do you like wine? Would you like to have the confidence to choose a wine to serve with a new recipe or an old favorite? Do you want to know where to begin when selecting a wine that makes your food taste better and the meal more enjoyable?"

"It's not difficult; in fact, it's fun! Of course, the more you learn about wine, the easier it becomes. You can begin by asking the advice of your fine wine shop or reading the wine description, but ultimately, you must learn to taste for yourself and to trust your own judgement. *If it tastes good to you, it is good!*"

These suggestions were written by Karen Keehn and I could find no better person to write an introduction to wine and food than Karen. She and her husband, Rich, own McDowell Valley Vineyards, an estate winery in Mendocino County, in Northern California. They are frequent visitors to Aspen. It is said of the Keehn's, "They don't just grow grapes and make good wine, they create varietal wines in a style to complement food and they know just which foods enhance which wines best, because they are constantly trying different combinations." (Millie Howie, *The Review* 1986.)

I have asked Karen, as a great cook and wine expert, to write some facts linking wines to food; a wonderful combination when used to enhance each other.

The Interested Consumer's Guide to Wine and Food.

WINE HAS FIVE PRIMARY STRUCTURAL COMPONENTS THAT AFFECT THE WAY FOOD TASTES:

1. FLAVOR   What flavor do I taste? Is it a fruit or berry, herb or spice (which are contributed from the grape itself) or vanilla, nut-like, oily or buttery (that comes from the way the wine was made)? How strong or how delicate is the flavor? Do I want to repeat a similar flavor in the food or use something that contrasts but does not compete with the wine?

2. ACIDITY   What level of acidity does the wine have? Is it low (lacking "zing"), balanced, crisp or tart? Wine acids peak food flavors, and "cut" the fat content of foods. Try using citrus instead of vinegar to enhance wine acids.

3. SWEETNESS   Is this a dry wine or does it have some level of sweetness? How much? Wines with sweetness tend to taste better with foods that have some sweetness, tartness, or saltiness. Dry wines tend to taste sour with sweet foods.

4. TANNIN   What is the level of tannin? Tannin (usually in fine red wines) is recognized by a puckering, dry sensation in the mouth like very strong tea. Its presence is necessary for wine to age and will be more noticeable in younger wines. Strong tannins can detract from delicate foods or combine with salt or acids to taste metallic. However, when these same wines are paired with foods higher in fat content (lamb, beef, duck, butter, cheese, etc.), their tannins seem to "bind" with the fat and "release" the fruit flavors in the wine.

5. STYLE   Style is the sum of flavor, acidity, sweetness, and tannin and is determined by the way the wine is made or processed. When

. . . .

matching wines and foods, *style may be as important as the variety of grape used to make the wine.* A wine grape variety can be made in many styles. Chardonnay, for instance, can be made with a clear perception of fruit, crisp acidity, some sweetness, and no oak complexity. Or, that same grape can be fermented in barrels for oak complexity with balanced acidity and no sweetness to produce a Chardonnay of a completely different style. Both may be excellent wines but the different styles will complement different foods.

Karen has provided the following wine descriptions. She prefaces them with saying, "These descriptions reflect the most common style from premium wineries. We believe that seasoning can be the tie that binds the food to the wine."

CHARDONNAY. The Chardonnay grape makes the world's finest dry wines. The fruit often conveys complex flavors of melon, pear, fig, apple or grapefruit with touches of honey and clove. The style is most often dry with rich fruit flavors and good acid structure complexed by a toastiness from fermentation or aging in small oak barrels. Other styles can be less assertive in flavor with a more pronounced acid structure.

SAUVIGNON BLANC/FUMÉ BLANC. Sauvignon Blanc's taste characteristics are often described as melon, pear, gooseberry or grapefruit; it can sometimes have vegetal, spicy or herbal overtones. This versatile white wine is most frequently made in a dry style with balanced acidity, complex fruit flavors and a touch of oak. Sauvignon Blanc is sometimes made with a light sweetness and no oak complexity.

CHENIN BLANC. This delicate white wine's charm lies in its subtle melon and pear flavors. It can be fermented to dryness with a balanced acidity and a touch of oak complexity. Other styles may be sweeter or more acidic with no oak complexity.

RIESLING or COLOMBARD. The Colombard can be similar to a Riesling wine with fresh, lively but delicate apple aromas and flavors. It should have a crisp, refreshing acidity to balance the usual hint of sweetness.

ZINFANDEL BLANC/WHITE ZINFANDEL. This wine has an appealing pale rose color with lively fruit flavors reminiscent of watermelon and spice. It is usually enhanced by a slight sweetness and a refreshing tartness. This popular blush wine category can vary in levels of sweetness and acidity, and is popular as an apéritif.

GRENACHE. A beautiful ruby red-colored wine with complexed flavors similar to strawberry and cherry. A delicious wine when made with just a touch of sweetness and good acidity; it serves as one of the most versatile wines with food.

CABERNET SAUVIGNON. The world's most noble red wine having a deep ruby color with distinctive, pungent aromas of black currant, raspberry, cherry, with touches of cinnamon, cedar and pepper. Premium styles may be more tannic when young to provide the necessary structure for aging. Its complexities and elegance are enhanced with bottle age.

SYRAH. Syrah is a wine of deep purple color when young, intense aromas and rich flavors of plum, blackberry and currant. Tannins are balanced with rich fruit, showing great finesse and complexity with age. The Petite Sirah, a different but similar variety, has cherry-like flavors, heavier tannin and pepper spice.

ZINFANDEL. Zinfandel is a ruby red wine with appealing raspberry flavor complexed by spiciness and hints of bay leaf and herb. Usually made in a readily drinkable style, it is also made as a light Beaujolais, heavy red or even a port style depending on the winery.

THE DO'S AND THE DON'TS OF COMBINING FOOD AND WINE

The DO's—to make pairing more enjoyable and less traumatic, we suggest that you adhere to a few basic concepts:

1. Try to strike a balance between the wine and food so that they each taste better when tasted together. To do this remember:
a. Stronger flavored wines seem to taste better when balanced with stronger flavored foods.
b. Conversely, more delicately flavored wines are better appreciated when served with foods that are more delicately seasoned or textured.
c. Wines with spicier aromas and flavors are often enhanced by similar spicy accents in foods; to carry this further, wines with bolder, coarser flavors are better matches for coarser, simpler fare.
2. When developing a recipe or deciding on a dish to pair with wine, it sometimes helps to think that most foods have little flavor of their own that enhances or competes with wine. Rather, foods serve as a base flavor or medium to carry other seasonings that can be matched to a wine variety or style. These seasonings can be the key to tying the wine & food flavors together.
3. Learn to use specific herbs, spices and seasonings to enhance certain wine varieties or styles. Examples: marjoram butter with fish & Fumé Blanc; beef with tarragon sauce and Cabernet Sauvignon; lamb with rosemary and Syrah.
4. Use the "beverage" wine as a cooking ingredient in sauces, etc. It really doesn't take much wine and it reinforces the same flavors in the food that are in the wine. If this sounds too inconvenient or expensive, you can use a wine of similar flavor, structure or style.
5. When serving more than one wine variety or style, we suggest that you progress from cold to room temperature, dry to sweet, white to rosé then red, delicate to bold, old to young.

6. Serve more simple foods with older wine vintages to better appreciate their complexities and elegance.

The DON'Ts—to avoid being disappointed, we advise a few words of caution when working with fine wine:

1. Wine that does not taste good enough to drink should not be considered good enough to cook with. The "off" flavors are often transferred to the dish.

2. Excessive use of some seasonings can overpower the taste & pleasure of wine. These include salt, garlic, vinegar, ginger, sugar, hot peppers & cilantro. Don't avoid using them altogether, just use with some restraint. Or combine with milder ingredients to "cut" their strength.

3. Vegetable acids can compete with wine. Many vegetables have acids that compete with the pleasures of wine, particularly artichokes, asparagus, spinach and sorrel. We suggest diminishing the competitive effect of their acids by using sweet spices or sauces containing cheese, cream, mayonnaise or other dairy products.

4. Cold temperatures subdue wine aromas & flavors. Temperatures that are too cold (below 55 degrees Fahrenheit) can subdue the aromas and flavors of more complex wines.

The pleasures of our palate are a complex interaction of flavors and aromas that are never perceived in isolation. Wine alone has over two hundred different aroma compounds. In this context we would like to suggest that it is a good practice to *serve the wine first* to savor its various flavors and impressions and *then* serve the food. In this way, each can be appreciated for its own enjoyment and then together. And, if you should choose a combination that delights all the senses together...Voila! Our heartiest thanks and congratulations.

Karen & Rich Keehn, PROPRIETORS
McDowell Valley Vineyards

RECIPE INDEX

NOTES

ORDER FORMS

To: Jill Sheeley, Box 845, Aspen, Colorado 81612

Please send me_____copies of **"Tastes of Aspen"** at $16.95 per copy.

($14.95 plus $2.00 for shipping) Enclosed is my check for $_____.

Name_____

Street_____

City_____ State_____Zip_____

☐ This is a gift. Please send directly to:

Name_____

Street_____

City_____ State_____Zip_____

- ✂

To: Jill Sheeley, Box 845, Aspen, Colorado 81612

Please send me_____copies of **"Tastes of Aspen"** at $16.95 per copy.

($14.95 plus $2.00 for shipping) Enclosed is my check for $_____.

Name_____

Street_____

City_____ State_____Zip_____

☐ This is a gift. Please send directly to:

Name_____

Street_____

City_____ State_____Zip_____